T.A.O.S.

The Art Of Skiing

Jerome S. Gladysz

T.A.O.S.: The Art Of Skiing

© 2002 by Jerome S. Gladysz

All rights reserved.
Printed in the United States of America.

No part of this book may be used or reproduced in any form whatsoever without written permission, except in brief quotations embodied in articles and reviews.

For information write:
Market Relations Press
6532 Castle Pines Rd.
Ft. Worth, TX 76132
817.732.2081

ISBN 0-963-88411-5   15.95
Library of Congress

Cover Design and Typography: Alan Carey Earle
Copy Editing: Paul Conant

Table of Contents

Introduction
    Preface 8
    Foreword: T. A. O. S.: The Art Of Skiing 10
    Contributors 13
        Jean Mayer 13
        Gordon Briner 14
        Alain Veth 15
        Jeff Mugleston 16
        Doug DeCoursey .17
        Debbie Armstrong 18
        Jerry Gladysz 20

First Run: Taos — The Experience — To answer the question, "What's so special about Taos?" 23
    Chapter 1: Why Taos Ski Valley Is Unique 24
    Chapter 2: The Last Bastion 27
    A Brief History Of Taos Ski Valley 28

The Second Run: Soul Skiing — The most important reason to go to the mountain 31
    Chapter 3: The Soul Skier 32
    Chapter 4: Skiing Enhances Your Life 34
    Chapter 5: If You Can Ski Taos 36
    Chapter 6: Focus On The Joy 38

The Ridge 101

Sixth Run: Bump Masters — Confidence dictates the activity 103
- Chapter 32: Edge First 105
- Chapter 33: Bend Your Knees, Watch Out For The Trees 107
- Chapter 34: Bumps Are All About Options 108
- Chapter 35: The Next Pole Plant 109
- Chapter 36: Release The Edge 111
- Chapter 37: S Not Z 112
- Chapter 38: A Different Focus – Weighting, Balance and Absorption 113
- Chapter 39: Something You Don't Have To Do . .115
- *Trail Names* 116

Seventh Run: Adventure Skiing — The everlasting search for fresh, untracked powder and soul 123
- Chapter 40: Adventure Skiing Is Self-Reliance . . .124
  - Never Turn Off Your Brain 124
- Chapter 41: Break Trail For The Tail 127
- Chapter 42: The Powder And The Resistance . .129
  - The Porpoise Turn .130
  - The Jump Turn 130
  - The Ski As A Tool .131
- Chapter 43: Move With The Mountain 132

Chapter 44: Timing Is Everything 133
Chapter 45: Bite A Piece Of Freedom 135
   Gullies Are Fun 135
   Look For Spaces Not Trees 136
   A Simple Commitment Move 137
Chapter 46: A Bag Of Tricks 138
Chapter 47: Shape Your Turn For
Adventure Skiing 140
Chapter 48: Equipment Helps 142
Chapter 49: Adventure Is More Rewarding 144
I finally made it 145

Eighth Run: The Kids — A learning machine 147
  Chapter 50: For Children, Learning Must Be Fun 148
  Chapter 51: Center On Learning 150
  Chapter 52: Separate The Parents
  From The Kids 152
   Only Once 153
   Have A Decent Breakfast 154
  Chapter 53: Children's Progression 155
   Early Prime Time 156
  Chapter 54: Children Are Natural Athletes 157
  Chapter 55: Children Learn Through
  Their Bodies 159
  Chapter 56: The Role Of The Parent
  In Children's Skiing 161

Chapter 57: How Long Is Best 163
Wow, It Does Look Like Fun! 165

Ninth Run: Late Bloomers — Motivated by the aura, the majesty, and the thrill 169
  Chapter 58: Be Flexible 170
  Chapter 59: Cognitive And Comfortable 172
  Chapter 60: Escape Versus Anxiety 174
    The Good 174
    The Bad 175
    The Helpful 175
  Chapter 61: A Balanced And Agile Style 176
  Chapter 62: Enjoy The Experience 178
    The Mecca Myth 179
  I Can't Believe I Skied The Steeps 180

Tenth Run: The New Equipment — Allows you to do more than ever before 183
  Chapter 63: Shorter Is Better 184
  Chapter 64: It May Be Easier, And It Sure Is Better 185
  Chapter 65: More Natural, And Sometimes Less Physical 187
    Proper Fitting 188
    Equipment For Children 188
  Chapter 66: Park and Ride — A Misnomer 190

    Extend Your Arc 191
    Edge Early 191
  Chapter 67: Athleticism Disguised 192
    Physically, Don't Cheat Yourself 193
    The Big WHY And The Big WHAT 193
    Stir Your Juices 194

Eleventh Run: High Performance Skiing — The mental aspects are most important 197
  Chapter 68: Visual Imagery — See Yourself 198
  Chapter 69: Plan Your Run 200
  Chapter 70: Fear Not .202
    And Seldom Was Heard A
    Discouraging Word 202
    Don't be Cueless 204
  Chapter 71: A Fearsome Focus 206
  Chapter 72: A Goal Habit 208
  Chapter 73: You Didn't Know You Weren't
  Supposed To Win 210
  Chapter 74: The Gold Of Sarajevo 213
  Down The Hill With Debbie 215
Index 216

Photo Credits:
Jeff Caven Photography — p. 13, 86, 146, 168; TSV — p. 14, 16, 22;
Alain Veth — p. 15; Doug DeCoursey — p. 17; Spike Mattford — p. 18;
Gittings — p. 20; Ken Gallard — p. 30, 42, 62, 102, 122;
Salomon — p. 180; Michael Holmquist — p. 196

Preface

Art transmits the highest feelings of man, implying a personal, unanalyzable creative power. Skiing, as taught by Taos Ski Valley, champions the artistic dimension of the science of ski instruction and gives it undeniable clarity and meaning. This book is a collection of skiing tips and philosophy attributed to Jean Mayer, Gordon Briner, Jeff Mugleston, Alain Veth and Doug DeCoursey, the principal architects of the nationally famous ski program; they typify the intense professionalism and skill level of the instructors at Taos Ski Valley. Debbie Armstrong, Giant Slalom Gold Medalist at the Sarajevo Olympics, also contributes vital thoughts on mental aspects of high-performance skiing.

Although this is not the "official" or "approved" manual, it does accurately reflect why so many have enjoyed Taos Ski Valley and consider its ski school to be the best in the country.

First, a couple of thoughts on how to read this book:

Sit back and relax.

Do not speed read. Try rolling the words around in

your mind, then swallow the thought.

Lots of specifics are not here. Lots of ideas are.

Many concepts are repeated; that's because they are important.

Read the book in one sitting but keep it as a reference when you go to the mountain. The stimulation and mental preparation of reading the appropriate run can change your approach to skiing and your entire day.

Essentially each chapter is a sound bite for your ski life — you'll ski the light.

Consider each discussion as a chat among friends, these diamonds only you can polish.

You'll end up with a good feeling, just like skiing Taos.

T.A.O.S.: The Art Of Skiing.

In New Mexico and in most ski states, every skier accepts the dangers inherent in the sport, and assumes the individual responsibility for knowing the range of his or her own ability — maintaining reasonable control of speed and course at all times while skiing. This book is intended to be an inspiration and a supplement to, but not a substitute for, personal instruction by a trained and qualified ski instructor.

One more thing: your equipment must be in excellent and safe condition. Have it checked regularly by a trained ski shop technician.

Art is science made clear.

Jean Cocteau, Le Coq et L'Arlequin

Contributors

Jean Mayer

Jean Mayer, Taos Ski School Technical Director, has guided the ski technique taught at Taos Ski Valley for the last forty-five years. Ernie Blake, TSV's legendary founder, recruited Jean from Bavaria from the U.S. Army's Ski School at Garmisch-Partenkirchen, after an amateur career as the French National Junior Champion. Jean created one of the first European-style learning systems in the U.S. and also the reputation for TSV as the premier ski school in the country — recognized best in the country two times by national media.

"Our mountain should offer a sanctuary, a haven for people who come here from all walks of life. And it is our responsibility to see that you find the escape, the refuge, and the joys of basic, natural life that you are looking for." Jean has championed the fun, joy, friendship, excitement and the rewards of self-discovery through skiing for forty-five years at Taos Ski Valley.

Gordon Briner

Gordon Briner is the General Manager of Taos Ski Valley. Prior to Taos, Gordon was the Director of Operations at Breckenridge, Colorado; Director of Skier Services and Ski School Operations at Keystone Resort and Arapaho Basin, Colorado; and Examiner for the Rocky Mountain Ski Instructors Association. He was instrumental in the initial founding of the Phil and Steve Mahre Training Centers at Keystone.

Gordon grew up in the skiing world and raced in the US Ski Association and at Fort Lewis College, Colorado. He represented the Rocky Mountain Division at the National Demonstration Team Try-outs and was President of the Board of Directors of Rocky Mountain Ski Instructors Association from 1978-1980.

"Our passion for the mountain and our unparalleled approach to learning," said Gordon, "presents skiing as an art form. It is a pure skiing experience that you'll only have in Taos."

Alain Veth

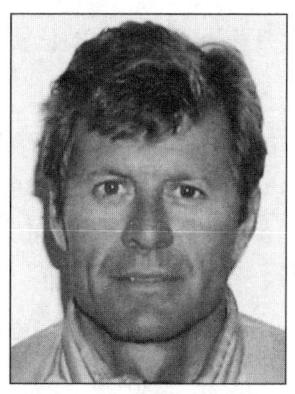

Alain Veth has been the major designer of the current Super Ski Week program at Taos Ski Valley. "The instruction is not an academic exercise but rather a hands-on and ski-through experience to expand your personal skills on the snow and your appreciation of the mountain." Alain's career includes many French national championship titles in slalom and giant slalom as a member of the French National Ski Team. Alain was also a ski technician for three years on the U.S. Women's World Cup Ski Team for the Women's World Cup (1988—1990), the Olympics (1988) and the World Ski Championship in Vail (1989).

Before coming to Taos Ski Valley, he was associated with Les Deux Alpes Resort in France and Silverstar in British Columbia. In France and the United States, Alain received Full Certification as a ski instructor and coach (PSIA and USSCA Level III). His racing championship awards and placements have established Alain as one of the world's best.

Currently Alain, in addition to his duties as head coach of the Super Ski Week and other ski instruction duties, is the proprietor of Le Ski Mastery in Taos Ski Valley, specializing in ski sales, tuning, and rentals.

Jeff Mugleston

Jeff Mugleston is one of the Ski School Managers at Taos Ski Valley. A sixteen-year veteran with a PSIA Level-3 Certification in Alpine and Nordic Downhill, Jeff served in a variety of capacities from instructor, trainer, Junior Elite 2 Manager, Taos Ski Team Coach and supervisor. He was also associated with Red River and Santa Fe, New Mexico and Treble Cone, New Zealand.

"It is the spirit of adventure of Taos that truly separate us from the rest. We take precise techniques proven by the best skiers in the world and deliver them in an way that is not only remembered but easily internalized. It is an art how Taos touches more than skiing — it is an experience."

Doug DeCoursey

Doug DeCoursey is a veteran instructor in the Ski School of Taos Ski Valley. For over twenty years Doug has served in a variety of capacities including supervisor, Mogul Mastery Coach, PSIA Training Coach, PSIA Examiner, and lecturer at the "Tech Talk" Presentation Series for Ski Week attendees. He also authored the book, *Visual Skiing (Doubleday, 1990)*, was a guest writer for *Snow Country Magazine* and other skiing publications, and is a frequent lecturer on ski history and technique. Prior to Taos, Doug instructed at Greek Peak, NY; Bolton Valley, VT; Steamboat Springs, CO and Ski Apache, NM.

"We can write endlessly about skiing on the steep terrain and the different conditions that exist in Taos. However, these are a learned activity for experienced skiers," Doug said. "Can you imagine trying to learn to swim out of a book, and then jumping into the deep end of a swimming pool? Well, this information is to inspire and help you visualize how to improve your skiing. But, for the ultimate benefit, join us on the mountain where we can really expose you to the art of advanced skiing at Taos."

Debbie Armstrong

On February 13, 1984 in Sarajevo, Yugoslavia, Debbie Armstrong exploded onto the international sporting scene with her Gold Medal performance in the Giant Slalom event of Alpine Skiing in the Winter Olympics. Debbie raced as a member of the United States Ski Team and competed on the World Cup circuit from 1981—1988.

Originally from Seattle, Washington, Debbie moved to Albuquerque, New Mexico following her retirement from international competition in 1988. After receiving her BA degree in History from the University of New Mexico, Debbie decided to return to the ski industry and is currently the Ambassador of Skiing at the Taos Ski Valley in New Mexico. Her interests include skiing and ski instruction, spending time with her family, camping, climbing, fishing and just about all sports. Debbie has been active in a variety of community service and charitable activities, including Global Relief Sarajevo. The goal of this reforestation project in war-torn Sarajevo is to raise funds and plant 300,000 trees to stabilize the surrounding hillsides of Sarajevo.

Debbie Armstrong's Skiing Highlights, Awards, Honors:
- US Ski Teams 1981—1988
- World Championship teams 1981, 1985, 1987
- Olympic teams 1984, 1988
- Gold Medal in the Giant Slalom, 1984, Sarajevo, Yugoslavia
- Sports Illustrated cover, February, 1984
- National Champion, Giant Slalom, 1987
- Honorary Chairperson for the Ski-For-All Foundation (a ski school for people with disabilities)

Jerry Gladysz

Once upon a time I was a helicopter pilot and found that type of intimate flying was an extraordinary experience. Then I discovered skiing as the next best thing to powered flight because it was the joy of effortlessly gliding down the hill in the rapture of nature's beauty. However, at Taos Ski Valley during a Super Ski Week, they exposed me to the art of skiing and a unique appreciation to what it can provide to the human spirit.

I have spent my entire professional life in advertising and public relations and found it impossible to sell anything that wasn't the real deal. Taos is the premier skiing location in North America. They have mastered the art of skiing and share it with all who come to visit. I hope you enjoy some of the thoughts presented here. See you on the slopes.

First Run:

Taos
– The Experience –

To answer the question, "What's so special about Taos?"

. . . a family-run philosophy, warm personal atmosphere, a skiing adventure.

. . . the best ski experience in the mountains.

"Taos is stimulating," said Debbie Armstrong, Giant Slalom Gold Medal Winner at the Sarajevo Olympics. "I love Taos Ski Valley because it is a very invigorating environment for me, from the level of the instruction, to the passion of the Ski School, to the mountain itself. I relish the opportunity to continue to learn and challenge myself while both technique and equipment are changing. Skiing is like life in the sense that it can never be totally mastered; there is always more to create with . . . like the snow . . . the weather . . . the speed . . . the mountain itself. That's what makes skiing so intriguing; it is all about the process."

1

Why Taos Ski Valley Is Unique.

Taos Ski Valley is the only major ski resort in operation today that is still 100% owned and operated by the same family who developed it. The friendly operation and the quaint, old-world ways of doing things contribute to the rustic charm of Taos versus the usual impersonal, corporate-giant operations with their glitzy, real estate developments and polished, strip-mall mentality.

A family-run philosophy also permeates the entire village of the Taos Ski Valley in that almost every business on the hill is an owner-operated enterprise. From ski shops to gift shops, hotels to restaurants, the owners are everywhere to make the valley more personal. Owner-operation on such a grand scale is a situation totally uncommon in the domestic ski industry today.

The warm personal atmosphere means that you can hook up with the locals to find your way around the mountain and discover new runs off the beaten path. Even the ability to strike up new acquaintances with other guests is easier because of the smallness of the resort and the resonance of the adventure. Whether it is the magic of the mountain or the sense of community of a family operation, both employees and visitors seem happier here. Smiles abound.

Lighting conditions also have an intangible effect on your mood and energy. At the base of the ski hill you will notice how different the sunlight reacts with the mountains that surround the valley. The angle of the sun in the southern latitude and its position relatively higher in the sky literally cause you to see things in a different light. Artists flock to the Village of Taos to make it an international art center because of the quality of the light and overall ambiance.

> **People don't come to Taos to be seen but to live life a little fuller and with more passion.**

People don't come to Taos to be seen but to live life a little fuller and with more passion. There is something about the sun, the snow and the mountain that brings out the soul of the skier. Taos is not pretentious, so feel free to dress down and be real.

The big-name skiers of most resorts are primarily attractions to build the image of the operation, but never to be skied with and only rarely seen. At Taos, the headliners are present every day, readily available to ski, wherever you want to ski. By the same token, the ski school classes explore all the challenging parts of the mountain including Blues, Blacks, Double-Blacks and the Ridge. It is a real adventure.

Taos is a skiing adventure that is not available in many other places. Relatively steep with untracked snow, it is as close to a backcountry experience as you will find in the boundaries of a ski area. One of the premier ways to enjoy this adventure-skiing wonderland is with the ski school to show you the way. Instruction from the technique standpoint or inspiration from the guide standpoint means "doing the mountain" is less stressful than ever before.

2

The Last Bastion

Taos is a ski area, not a winter resort complex, or a real estate development. Ernie Blake founded the area for real skiers to enjoy the best ski experience in the mountains. TSV provides a true ski experience, by showing people how to connect with this adventure through a world class ski school, in great snow, on a mountain as challenging as you want it to be. You don't have to be an expert to ski at Taos, yet there is no better place to become one.

To find out if you are right for Taos ask yourself a simple question, "Do I love to ski?" Regardless of your age, gender, ski ability, or physical shape, if you want to ski, Taos is for you.

If you want to ski, Taos is for you.

A Brief History
Of Taos Ski Valley

Ernie Blake and his Aleut friend, Peter Totemoff, had been eyeing the Twining area from the air for some time. The consistent snow cover impressed them. It appeared to arrive early in the fall and stay late into the spring. In May, 1954, they trudged through three feet of fresh powder to survey the area from the ground.

"This looks good," prophesied Ernie.

"This is impossible skiing terrain," responded Pete.

The "this" was a formidable and uninhabited wilderness. A few bleak frames of decaying log cabins, a derelict bullwheel from the old mining lift, and some battered ore buckets were all that remained from the abandoned 19th century copper mining outpost called Twining.

Nevertheless, with limited personal finances, no significant backers and three small children in tow (Mickey, 11, Wendy, 7, and Peter, 5), Ernie and Rhoda set out to create a ski resort from scratch. Closest friends and family advisors considered them completely mad.

It is difficult to imagine what Taos Ski Valley was like in 1955:

- There was not even a trace of a ski trail anywhere. It was so densely forested that a small cabin, 200 feet from the base, went undetected for two years.
- There was no customer base or any apparent skier interest in such a venture.

- There was no water except from the Rio Hondo.
- There was no electricity, which meant construction of any kind would have to be done without benefit of electrical power.
- The only road from Taos was a jeep trail barely one vehicle wide in places. It was an obstacle course plagued by rockslides and mud and frequently buried by enormous amounts of snowfall.
- There was no phone or mail delivery.

It's not surprising that for the first 18 years, Taos Ski Valley functioned in the red. Fortunately, profits were not the Blakes' main concern. As Wendy says, "More than anything else, Mom and Pops looked for a place where they would have the most fun skiing for the rest of their lives."

Ernie and Rhoda always insisted they started this area for their own pleasure. In later years Ernie wrote, "We tried to keep things simple. We never operated beyond our means or developed tastes that required vast sums of money that we didn't have. We still are about as far removed from a high-fashioned type of resort as you can find. All we've ever wanted here are people who took skiing seriously, who relish a personal and caring ski atmosphere in the true old-fashioned sense."

Change has been inevitable, but we hope certain things will never change. As Chris Stagg, Vice President of Marketing for Taos Ski Valley, says, "Taos has always been, and will always be, a place that does things a little differently."

Second Run

Soul Skiing

The most important reason to go to the mountain.

. . . harmonize with nature and blend with the elements.

. . . snow is the medium and the feeling achieves the renaissance.

. . . a new degree of body awareness.

. . . don't let ego get in the way of becoming a soul skier.

. . . listen to what your skis are saying and dance on the mountain.

3

The Soul Skier

All winter sport activities have changed more in the last decade than in the last forty years. Taos Ski Valley is still identified as a purist resort, maintaining its attitude toward traditional skiing and mountaineering as it does, but that is easy to do when you have a mountain and environment as pure and challenging as Taos. This also attracts the type of skier who appreciates those purist ideals, more of a soul skier than anything else.

A soul skier is one who harmonizes with nature and blends with the elements. This skier is not as much concerned with performance for performance sake as in harmonizing with the mountain, the slope, the terrain and the elements, thus skiing as a way of life. It is a spiritual and romantic concept more than anything.

Soul skiing is one of the most important reasons why people go to the mountain and the snow. Skiing is not like going to the state fair where you might buy a ticket and get to ride round and round on a Ferris Wheel. People come to the mountain and search for much more; it truly can touch your soul and your spirit.

"This magical spirit of skiing is what we try to instill in all our skiers," said Jean Mayer. "Lessons can develop your ability to glide on the snow, but our true objective is to enhance your experience on the mountain and the thrill of finding a new expression of yourself. People today crave anything that can add extra value to the precious little spare time that they have to spend with their loved ones, friends and even themselves." This time poverty affects everyone as they seek additional fulfillment from all in which they are involved. Skiing then takes its place as an extraordinary method to add a new texture to your quest for fulfillment because of all that it demands and provides in return.

Jean concludes, "The instructors at Taos Ski Valley take on a somewhat different role, more like a friend or coach to advise you in this new discovery of yourself and to help you blend with the elements."

a spiritual and romantic concept more than anything

4

Skiing Enhances Your Life

This book will discuss the basic fundamentals of skiing technique relative to current equipment, at whatever level you ski, as the technical foundation to support sound practice and breakthrough achievement. Sound practice is meant in the sense of making you more efficient on the snow. However, it is possible for you to achieve a breakthrough in your personal creativity, whether you are a beginner or an expert skier. This is all about personal creativity on the snow and how it will enhance your enjoyment of life.

Please note that all of this is presented within the context of your comfort zone. There is much here that will challenge you, but it should never threaten you.

Skiing is really an act of love with nature which gives to you unconditionally.

The mountain presents the opportunity to have fun through skiing where your body angles and balance allow you to experience the sensation of the freedom of gliding, weightlessness and defying gravity. What a sport! Both your mind and body come into play with your senses of sight, sound and touch producing your response. You put yourself in a challenging situation where no one else would go, in a snow storm or in the cold, and do it for fun.

Skiing is really an act of love with nature which gives to you unconditionally. You in return can be unconditional in your response, of course, at your own level. This is what the soul skiers at Taos come to find — that union with nature, themselves and their fellow man. The camaraderie and friendship between you and the instructors develop as they help you become a better skier. It is an honest affection for a common activity and the resulting self-enhancement that is so powerful. The reward achieved is beyond the material success but rather is only measured in the soul, mind and spirit. You have chosen the medium of snow and the feeling of skiing to achieve this renaissance.

5

If You Can Ski Taos

The majority of the guests coming to Taos Ski Valley think it is a very challenging ski resort. Taos is perceived to be a big purist mountain with steep terrain, for skiers who boast frequently, "If I can ski Taos, I can ski anywhere." That perception is somewhat exaggerated, because there are steep and challenging runs at almost every resort, just as there are many great intermediate and beginner runs at Taos. Other resorts don't expose the black runs immediately as when you first arrive at Taos and look up Al's Run, which is an monstrous array of bumps that seem to never end.

However the reality of Taos is that it is a purely awesome hill, complete with a breath-taking variety of runs, many of which are steep. The mountain has not changed to the whims of the current snow sports industry with real estate promotions. With no real estate to sell, Taos has a unique signature among ski resorts as one that has maintained its integrity and character. Here the art of skiing is alive and well among the soul skiers that inhabit these hills, steeps and valleys.

Why the emphasis on soul skiing? The concept of soul skiing is vital for your understanding of the art of skiing at Taos. Consider the Hawaiians who are notorious soul surfers: they surf for the love and the elegance of the water. They roll with the flow of the waves and harmonize with what the sea gives them. Many Europeans tend to be more aggressive in their pursuit of the sea pleasures and its bounty. In competitions this frequently manifests itself with the more aggressive person's interest in the result, whereas the soul surfer is only interested in the process.

> the mountain has not changed to the whims of the snow sports industry

Understanding this concept will help you understand the art of skiing. Most of the guests come to Taos with the expectation of not becoming Olympic champions but rather of getting to know, enjoy and love the mountain in addition to the experience of skiing. They want to achieve a new degree of body awareness to handle a variety of terrains and speeds successfully and to derive more pleasure from the hill. In other words, they want to have more fun.

6

Focus On The Joy

Since the art of skiing in Taos focuses on what makes you happy, instructors see a lot of problems from two sources: the first are those elements outside of yourself called previous instructors or incorrect information received; and second, those past negative ski experiences. Unfortunately the baggage car is usually full of those things that a previous instructor didn't do to make you a better skier, or perhaps the instructor's interpersonal skills were lacking, resulting in inspiration-killing attitudes such as being too demanding, or too controlling, not caring enough, too dogmatic, not gentle, not charitable or just too much ego. All of these don't make a happy skier.

The second problem area may simply reside in you, from the basics of impatience to the far more complicated concept of success for the sake of success. Many skiers are like mountain climbers who pay $50,000 to climb Mt. Everest and won't settle for anything less than reaching the top. Their obsession with that result causes them to sacrifice all reasonable care and safety standards while they try to achieve the goal, instead of enjoying the magnificent experience. In the same way, ego gets in the way of becoming a soul skier. Sometimes it is simply thinking you are better than you really are, or sometimes there is the personality that just can't be taught.

Ego gets in the way of becoming a soul skier.

At Taos, the journey is as important as the destination, in that the time spent leaves you filled with memories of the challenge, the fun, the camaraderie – the joy of the experience.

The Dangers Of A Purist

There are dangers from embracing these purist feelings because some people will actually resent you for them. Perfection has its price. These are the observations of Jean Mayer who has been involved with skiing as a life quest for more than fifty years. The views from this perspective are of the whole forest and not of each specific tree. Perspective is everything. Old wisdom admonishes you, the skier, to concentrate not on the trees but the space and path between the trees and your journey down the hill.

7

The Best Coach is Always With You

The better you listen and interpret what your skis are saying, the better you will be able to ski. In order to learn how to ski, you must listen to the coach that is always with you, your skis. The instructor acts as the interpreter to translate the messages you are receiving, such as, "that means you are too far forward on your skis," or "you are too far back," or "you are impatient."

Who dances on the mountain? Only those who ski in balance, in tune with their environment, very open to listening, feeling, hearing, smelling and using all of the sensations possible to interpret what is going on. You are more confident to leap from the intermediate to experience what an expert skier does, which is impossible unless you are willing to open yourself up to the sensations of the hill. Your fitness and knowledge help you to experience at the expert level, but being in touch with the hill fulfills the circle.

listen and interpret what your skis are saying

Taos "Disaster"
Enhances The Blake Legend

The Denver Post, January 9, 1977, by Frank Riley

Taos, N.M. — Of all the stories that have been told to create the Ernie Blake legend, none more accurately captures the essence of the man than what has been happening these past holiday weeks during a "disaster" grand opening at his New Mexico ski resort.

For the second time in 21 years, Ernie had to open without enough snow. There was 14 inches of snow on his slopes, more than at most resorts in the Rockies. And many a ski entrepreneur would have accented the positive in breathless prose.

But when asked about ski conditions Ernie Blake, in his characteristically rasping voice still rumbled with a few Swiss consonants, answered with the simple truth, "Well, put it like this – it's lousy. Cancel your reservation . . . stay home . . . have sex . . . do anything that's fun except come here and spend your money . . . ."

So, the lodges at Taos remained solidly booked for the New Year's weekend, as they have been for most of these past two decades. Ernie's friends knew that if the skiing continued to be lousy, the old maestro would compensate in other ways.

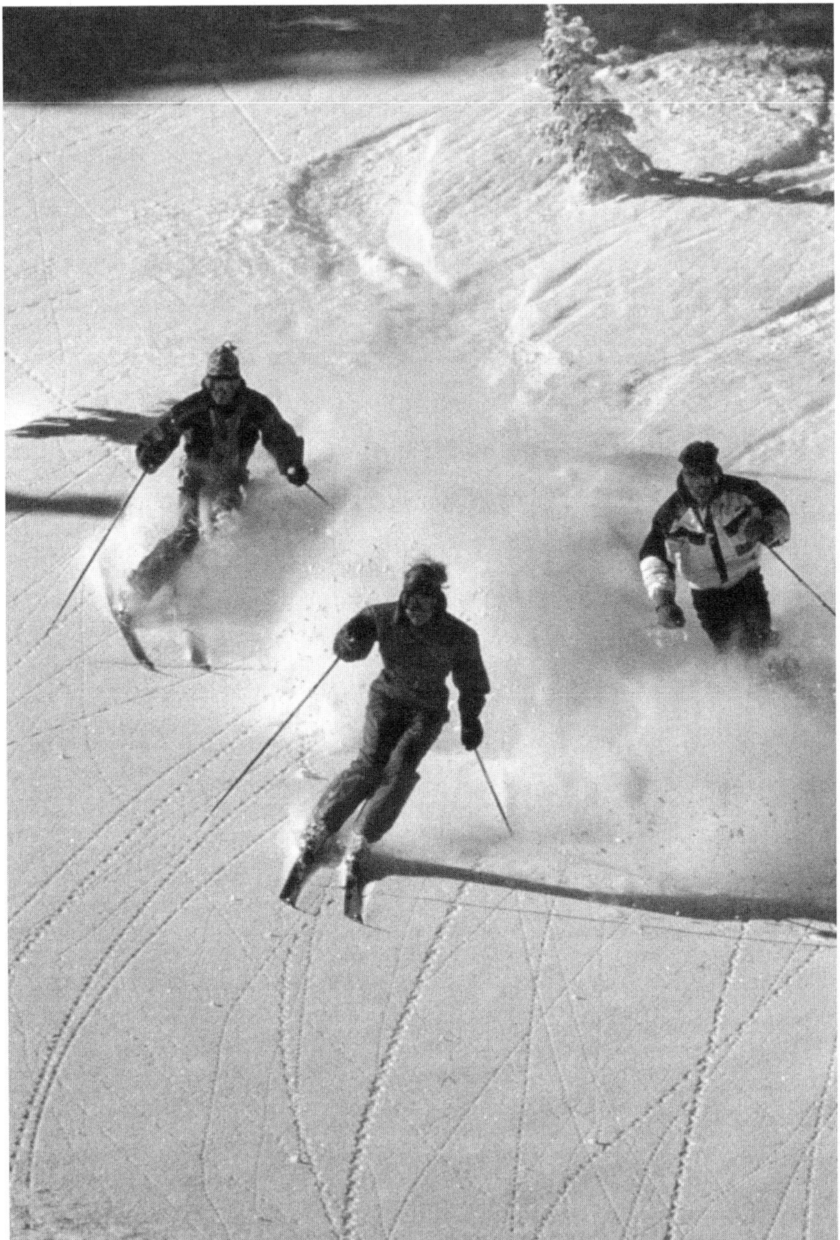

Third Run:

Ski School Required.

If you want to ski Taos, ski it with the ski school.

. . . the skier is the artist, the skis are the tools.

. . . for the best time of your life.

. . . Taos instructors are responsible for the accolades.

. . . they do things differently than other areas.

. . . you hold to what you create more than what you're told.

. . . the most relevant information about technical skiing.

. . . better to go through the actions than listening.

. . . everything is done to help the skier.

. . . see more than 51% of the total area.

"Jean Mayer is fond of saying, "The ski school makes sense for every level of skier — the beginner simply wants to get to the top of the mountain, whereas the intermediate would prefer to enjoy more of the adventure areas, while the expert wants to add versatility and experience all of the steeps available."

Whatever you hope to achieve in your skiing, chances are that Taos Ski Valley can help you get there. Jean says, "It doesn't matter at what level you ski, you first get control on the terrain that you want to ski, and then become more comfortable on the terrain that you want to ski, and ultimately achieve enough confidence to refine what you do on whatever terrain you want to ski." Improving your skiing is nothing more that going through that cycle, and refining your technique, on more and more challenging terrain.

8

The Experience Of The Mountain

The Ernie Blake Ski School at Taos Ski Valley is acknowledged to be a very fine school by the students; they love it so they come back and repeat it as a big part of their skiing life. A popular feeling is that if you ski Taos you have to ski it with the ski school, at whatever level of competence you are. Most resorts have predominantly beginners in their ski school program whereas Taos has a very high percentage of very good skiers on a regular basis. Most of the instructors who come from other areas to learn at the TSV Ski School envy it because so many high-level skiers are enrolled to share the experience of the mountain. The whole mountain experience is continually stressed to these instructors rather than confining their focus exclusively to movement around the bumps or down some steeps.

> **On the mountain, the skier is the artist; the skis are the tools.**

Each bump or terrain feature has many ways in which it can be navigated depending on the snow condition and the situation. You can never dictate to the mountain. A ski slope does not have the predictability of a bowling alley which is pretty flat, plays with a ball that is generally round, and pins that are more or less at the end of the lane. Skiing is artistic in the same way as is carving a piece of wood or stone. The sculptor must find the grain in the material to be better able to flow his work with his tools. On the mountain, the skier is the artist; the skis are the tools.

9

Ski School Required

When Taos Ski Valley first started operation, the lodge guests were required to take ski school lessons along with their lift tickets. This requirement was a practical necessity because the only lift up the hill was the Poma Lift up Al's Run, and Al's Run was also the only way down.

Ski lessons for their guests are still viewed as a practical necessity by most of the lodge owners who want their guests to come back. This is one of the magical reasons they return to the mountain — their experience is rewarding.

> **they had the best times of their lives during Ski Week**

Surveys of guests enrolled in ski school continually point out that they had the best times of their lives during Ski Week. Even in those rare instances of a thin base of snow, the ski students were able to find the best snow consistently and enjoy themselves thoroughly. If you view your time on the mountain as precious and your everyday responsibilities as burdensome and stressful, this incomparable adventure should be your escape.

10

Changing But Never Changing

Taos Ski Valley has never moderated its ski instruction philosophy of love for the sport and love for the mountain in order to maintain its position as one of the most respected ski schools in the country. However, the way that philosophy has been translated has changed and improved over time. It has become less dogmatic to fit the guests who now come far better prepared than ever before. The American public is in better condition physically and mentally for skiing.

Taos instructors are responsible for the accolades its ski program has achieved. A lot has always been demanded from them: mostly they must love the sport, care about what they are teaching, and improve themselves constantly. One must be first a good skier in order to become a good teacher. Taos Ski Valley doesn't stress the specific ways in which the instructors may translate the techniques to their students because if the instructors are turned on to the concept, they will find a way to share it with everyone.

Taos Ski Valley has been able to achieve this unusual

unity as a ski school because they appreciate each other's ideas and experiences while they have grown together. They all contribute and add value to the art of skiing which is TAOS.

its ski instruction philosophy of love for the sport

11

The Taos Experience

Skiing is an experience. You can increase the enjoyment of skiing by improving how you ski through the ski school and by having an opportunity to experience the best skiing environment on the mountain. More importantly, you'll be more aware of the other experiences you have while you are skiing and appreciate the total activity more. This is the pure skiing experience that you'll have in Taos.

Taos is uniquely able to establish a tangible connection between the skier and the mountain that one won't experience anywhere else. At the ski school, the staff really understands how to ski better and how to help you enjoy skiing more. Other areas may coddle and babysit their guests, starting with a gentle tour around the mountain, always making sure they don't get challenged too much. However when people come to Taos to be challenged by the experience and stretch themselves, TSV is happy to accommodate them.

a tangible connection between the skier and the mountain

The Ernie Blake Ski School has been consistently

rated as one of the top ski schools in the country not because they do the same thing better than anyone else, but rather because they do things differently than other areas. The difference is technical, physical and emotional, which by itself is different than anywhere else. It is a unique experience.

12

Emotional Gravitas

Like everything at Taos Ski Valley, the Ernie Blake Ski School is guest-centered. The school caters to the more adventuresome and athletic because of the terrain and simply the challenge of getting here. They don't orient the program to the lowest common denominator, so their standards are higher.

It is the spirit of adventure and the emotional "gravitas" of Taos that truly separate them from the rest. Jean Mayer, the Technical Director, has instilled a passion for skiing into the entire organization, always presenting precise technical concepts in the context of emotions. Emotions? What does emotion have to do with skiing? Everything. When precise techniques, proven by the best skiers around the world, are linked to the emotional benefits of your actions, you have something that is not only remembered but easily internalized. Whether the emotional response is created from romping in the snow,

> **You hold on to that which you create more than what you have been told.**

or screaming down the slope, or the breathtaking beauty of the mountains, you hold on to that which you create more than what you have been told. You benefit from emotional experiences and ideas more than any sterile presentation of technique or esoteric discussion. Taos touches more than skiing; it's an experience.

13

The Best Skiers About Skiing

Perhaps the most predominant attitude heard at the ski school is, "you're the expert, Taos, now make me better." Often the steeps hold the most allure for the aspiring experts because it is the key challenge associated with Taos Ski Valley. The basic theory is that they want to be challenged, to be stretched, to be what they want to be.

Taos Ski Valley has maintained a leadership position in the forefront of ski instruction as recognized by the guests who have received the instruction. It's not solely about teachers teaching, nor students learning, but rather the skiers' total experience. This is a remarkable feat considering that national surveys are a numbers game and Taos isn't the largest ski area, nor is its ski school the highest volume instruction operation. The attribution must be given to Jean Mayer, who has an incredible commitment to knowing the latest, most relevant information in technical skiing. His input comes directly from the mainspring of national ski teams and world class skiers to keep

it's the skiers' total experience

him several years ahead of everyone else when it comes to ski technique.

One of the most notable departures from accepted technique, even from the PSIA (Professional Ski Instructors Association) norm, was Jean's views on skiing stance and balance. For years there was a disparity between the nationally recommended technique and that of Taos.

Translating these advanced technical concepts into skiing instruction for the average skier is the real talent. After all, everyone can't be a world class slalom racer, but you can look for a way to enjoy your time on the hill more. Almost yearly, the technique taught by Taos Ski Valley is moderated somewhat, not change for change's sake, but improvement linked to reality.

14

Guided Into Learning

Adults learn better when they are guided into learning, even though they can be entertained by a discussion of the finer aspects of technique. But discussion is one thing and internalizing a technique is another. Understanding follows only when the ski concepts connect with motor skills. Since skiing is a physical activity, muscles must fire before the body will learn. That is why the mantra, "do this" or "do that" or "follow me", still prevails in the ski teaching lexicon because you are better off going through the actions than listening to any esoteric discussion of theory.

You also will never learn how to ski from a book, any book, including this one. However, books do expedite mental preparation by providing the reason why things work, which is still important to rational people.

Better off going through the actions than listening.

15

No Plateaus In Technique

A lot of ski instruction theory has taken the skier from beginner to intermediate as quickly as possible in order to get the skier up on the mountain and to feel comfortable skiing. The instruction was minimal, and the resulting technique was also equally modest.

constant refinements provide a natural progression

For example, the hockey stop is a good tool and the basis for a lot of technique, like the skidded turn or the Christie. Practically, it allows beginners to get up and off the hill with a minimum of instructions, enjoy more of the total mountain experience and fall in love with skiing.

One of the things that sets Taos ski instruction philosophy apart is the never-ending penchant for analyzing the top skiers to find out what makes them good. This also pertains to the equipment they use, because top skiers consistently serve as the vanguard of the manufacturers' design efforts.

These observations fuel constant refinements to ski technique that provides the beginner with a natural progression to prevent a plateau in the achievement level. Everything is done to help the skier toward the ultimate goal of expert skiing.

16

Adventure Skiing

Another of the core competencies of Taos is adventure skiing. Not only is there a lot of it with more than 51% of the total ski area, it is easy to access. Adventure skiing is one of the areas of instruction in which the Ski School excels, i.e., exposing you at whatever ability level you are to ski the ungroomed terrain, within your comfort zone. This area encompasses the moguls, trees, chutes, powder, steeps or whatever isn't flat or groomed.

at whatever ability level you are

The Martini Tree

Once upon a time, in the winter of 1957-58 in the tiny ski kingdom of Taos, King Ernst was not happy. He was burdened with a couple of fair young maidens in his ski class who had abandoned all hope of ever making it down the mountain on skis.

He cajoled. He yelled. He pleaded. He threatened. All to no avail.

Then, he spied his son, Prince Michael, skiing toward the class. "Michael, go tell your mother, the Queen, to mix up a batch of liquid courage and bring it to me. Ski quickly."

The Prince followed his father's orders and returned, in very good time, with the magic potion the Queen had prepared.

Not long after the ladies drank the potion, their failing spirits revived, turning them into skiing goddesses, at least in their own minds.

"Aha!" proclaimed the King. "I do believe I have stumbled upon a very clever device that shall become part of the teaching curriculum on my mountain." He sent forth a proclamation decreeing The Martini Tree would be the official tree of his kingdom.

Martini Trees were planted and thrived until lawyers, insurers, and litigious subjects began to threaten their very existence. Unhappily, all but one have vanished from the kingdom. That one is protected by one of the king's faithful retainers, Dan of the Iron Ring. Only he may reveal its location.

The End

"Not everyone who comes to Taos takes our ski week. But for those who don't the survival rate is low."

Ernie Blake, founder 1957

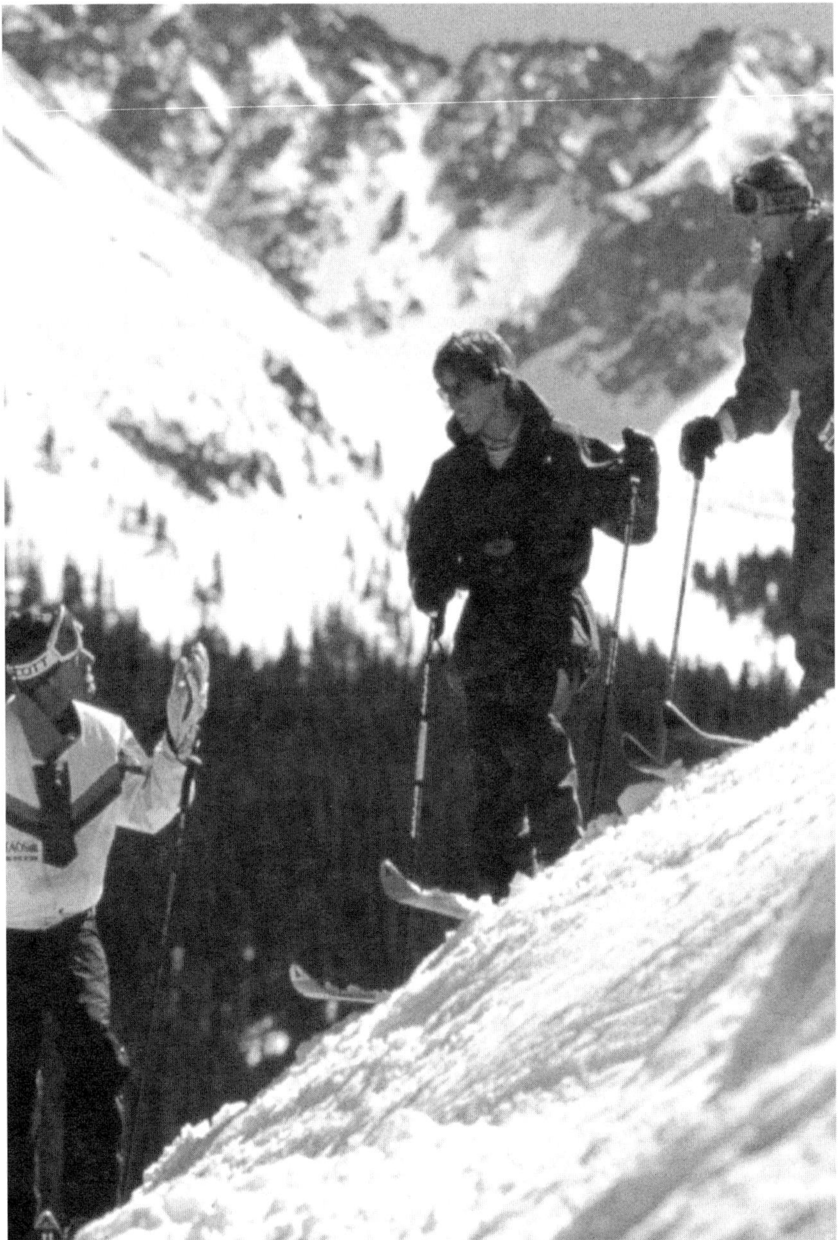

Fourth Run:

Ski Week Preferred

To improve your skiing and re-energize your spirits.

. . . make the concept your own.

. . . if you deepen your experience you are more likely to return.

. . . you learn through your own learning style.

. . . learn the "why" and the "how" of performance.

. . . total immersion will make you a better skier.

. . . a hands-on, ski-through experience expands personal skills.

. . . you mimic great technique artfully demonstrated.

. . . your deficiencies are exposed, your motivations are increased.

. . . not merely how to turn better but how to improve your life.

17

Experience And Adventure

The Ski Week programs are an experience and an adventure unique to Taos Ski Valley. Undoubtedly, there are other resorts with multi-day, ski instruction programs, but only Taos has the extraordinary ingredients to make it an adventure. Start first with the mountain, incomparable in its variety of terrain and its ability for fun. This mountain naturally draws a type of skier who demands the caliber of instruction necessary to handle challenges afforded by this terrain. This simple combination for adventure is completed with the natural intensity of Ski Week and great gobs of camaraderie to create a truly memorable experience.

TSV has created two approaches to this ski instruction program that differ in intensity. The regular Ski Week program works well for most people, comprised of five or six days in a row, morning lessons, in small groups, with the afternoon free to do what they want. For some people, they practice in the afternoon what they learned in the morning, for others they simply ski with a friend, family member or go to town. The Ski Week program allows people to improve their skiing and more importantly to enjoy themselves, and re-energize their spirits. On the other hand, the Super Ski Week program is for those who want to be totally immersed in ski technique, with lessons both in the morning and the afternoon, for six days in a row.

In the regular Ski Week program, the Ski School also accommodates some homogeneous groups, such as women, children and those over sixty. For example, in Women's Ski Week, women can choose to ski with groups of women in a program fitted to their ski ability levels. Or in the Master's Ski Week, men and women can choose to ski in groups of individuals over sixty, also according to their individual ability levels. Each of these special groups has a clear picture of what will be most helpful to them specifically.

Make The Concept Your Own

The core concept of the Ski Week experience centers around time for discovery. There is no substitute for time in a training program. For the student to learn, time is not a luxury but a necessity for listening, trying, adapting and retrying the skills. Time

> **There is no substitute for time in a training program.**

then allows discovery of how the technique works when you apply it, to your body, with your experience, at your ability level and in the conditions on the hill. Discovery means making the concept your own.

18

Was He Nuts?

When Ernie Blake first came to Taos, most people politely said he was nuts. They said that the slopes were way too steep and people wouldn't come to ski this kind of terrain. To further exacerbate the situation, for the first three years of the Taos ski area operation, the only trail down was Al's Run. Snake Dance soon followed, and after a couple of more years Porcupine became the easiest way down. The practical necessity of getting people off the mountain made Ernie realize the importance of developing a great ski school that could improve his guests' technique and allow them to enjoy it enough to return. Success depended upon people enjoying skiing on terrain they never imagined could be this steep.

Success depended upon people enjoying skiing.

Ernie then convinced the lodge owners to offer the ski school "package" along with the lift tickets. As a matter of practical necessity, the early lodges did not give the guest the option of buying a lift ticket only, but required participation in the ski school because they understood how important it was for the guest to enjoy the hill and the experience.

10 X More Likely

One indicator of the guest attitude toward Ski Week is that participants are ten times more likely to return than a non-ski school guest. This is another example of the vision of the founder proving correct. At the time, it seemed absurd to require the guest to take ski lessons, yet history has proven that those who did enjoyed their skiing so much more, that they returned year after year to repeat the experience.

The avowed intention of ski school is to deepen your experience in addition to your enjoyment of the mountain, and the years of returning Ski Week guests prove that idea true. This is another reason why Taos Ski School is recognized as one of the premier ski schools in the country.

19

The Benefit of Time

In the learning-centered approach of Ski Week, the instructors have the benefit of time to recognize how people learn, whether it is kids, adults, teens, women or masters. Once your learning pattern is identified by the instructors, they approach what you need to learn through your learning style, rather than through their teaching style. That's how the benefit of time helps them find out what will work for you and what won't.

In the Ski Week Program, the camaraderie achieved in a small group is like having another instructor there, because you have one thing to learn but may have several different approaches to hear and see it taught. By presenting a point many ways, the instructor seeks different avenues to appeal to the different people present, and frequently one person learns while another person is being taught.

time helps them find out what will work for you

20

The Ski Experience – Different Each Week

Each Ski Week program is different each week in that it is designed around the needs and goals of each of the guests that make up each group. Invariably, the first day is spent in a variety of snow and slope conditions in order to understand everyone's aspirations. At first, Ski Week started with a simple "ski-off" to determine the student groups, based on ability level. Now, in addition to the ability level, groups are further delineated by intensity and hopes for the week. A tone for each group also develops: some just want to have fun and tour the mountain, while a few are more intensely centered on technique, yet others want the adventure of trees and steeps. The first day frequently previews some of the terrain identified in the guests' objectives.

> **delineated by intensity and hopes**

Camaraderie

At the same time, you have the opportunity to make sure

you are comfortable with the group and its goals. Camaraderie and team spirit are definite assets to maximize the benefits of the program. The depth of the bond among team members is remarkable – it develops from the love of this unique sport experience and commonality of purpose, whether it is adventure or instruction. Friendships that develop on a ski slope seem to last a lifetime. Alternative group placement is available anytime to accommodate individual chemistry within the group or with the instructors.

Day two of Ski Week typically addresses the fundamental techniques necessary to accomplish some of the objectives of the group. **the bond is remarkable** For example, if your group wants to ski The Ridge and the chutes, then the basics of a jump turn, kick turn or traverse may be in order. Whereas if the trees are your cup of tea, then some practice in the powder or some time on the moguls may be appropriate. And then of course, if a storm brings powder, most schedules will be changed to take advantage of the opportunity.

Why And How

In the first part of the week, the program builds to your expectations and provides the techniques required to achieve them. The seeds of knowledge are planted with the "why" philosophy and stimulated to grow with the "how" experience. By midweek, the schedule sharpens its focus to address all the items on each participant's agenda and to click with you in your own way.

The second part of the week overlays practical tactics on top of sound technique. A good foundation is required for both creative as well as practical skiing. For example, those runs that you attempted during the reconnaissance runs earlier in the week can now be explored with a whole new attitude of confidence.

Ski Week must be dynamic and versatile because of the uncertainty of the weather and the composition of the groups themselves. It would be a mistake to follow an agenda irrespective of how it applies to your concerns and the quality of your total experience. Yet demonstrating a new move or position is never enough by itself to generate improvement in skiing performance, but rather it takes a dynamic intellectual and physical connection to make a difference.

Your attitude as you approach the slopes is the next essential ingredient to be considered. If you are fearful, you may not be able to apply a technique even if you have practiced it. Your mental state as a skier must be up to the run you are considering in order for you to release the technique required to experience it successfully.

see Debbie Armstrong's comments, Chapter 70: Fear Not

Learning Versus Performance

Ski Week also touches on the concept of the learning zone versus the performance zone of the skier. You must be aware of what your arousal level is in order to reach peak performance: for some it is the quiet calm that is necessary before the storm; and for others, it is the adrenalin high of physical stimulation that fills the bill. There is a big difference between the zone in which you learn and the zone in which you perform. Peak performance is rarely achieved in a learning mode. The structure of Ski Week focuses first in the learning zone, then comfortably expands the performance zone to extract the benefits of what you learn.

Even the nights of Ski Week have some optional educational activities to enlighten and inspire you. From a technical discussion of new equipment and technique, to snow safety and a history of Taos Ski Valley, there is information available to provide a new dimension to your adventure.

At the conclusion of the Ski Week experience, you will have an inescapable conclusion that you have learned something and that you want to learn more. Perhaps you may even notice a subtle, personal transformation that takes place which could be referred to as the *soul-skier* effect. Instructors report this phenomenon as follows:

skiers arrive all wound up and in a mind frame with very high expectations; skiers leave with expectations totally fulfilled but at an entirely different intensity level. With the new calmness is a different energy level and reappraisal of goals . . . what you thought you wanted may not seem that important anymore.

Peak performance is rarely achieved in a learning mode.

21

Twelve Years Of Super Ski Week

Super Ski Week has been a permanent feature of the Taos Ski Valley ski program. This is a total immersion program of morning and afternoon lessons, for six consecutive days, with small groups of students, selected by skill and intensity levels. The curriculum is made up of a number of learning experiences that include drills, gates, bumps, GS and slalom racing, crud, powder in addition to the Ridge. Each of these environments immerses you in situations that emphasize balance, technique and all-around agility to make you a better skier.

Drills are used to internalize the learning points and over the years, new drills have been added, modified or eliminated by the new equipment. For example, one drill uses stubbies, or short, flexible poles at a height just below the knees, to show you how to set up an edge early, work on your line down the hill and help you to commit to the type of quick turns necessary in some situations. The simple, practical

emphasize balance, technique and all-around agility

application for this is in a bump run, when you can follow your line and go from top to bottom nonstop.

22

Super Intensity

Intensity is the name of the game in Super Ski Week. It can't be any other way when you are immersed in a learning environment, with the top instructors, for five to six hours a day, six days in a row. The instruction is not an academic exercise but rather a hands-on and ski-through experience to expand your personal skills on the snow and appreciation of the mountain.

Intensity also pertains to the commitment of the instructor cadre which is specially selected, from the head coach through all the instructors, and dedicated to the belief that they can guarantee a skiing understanding breakthrough with each of the guests in the program. The supervisors have been known even to pull people out of the group for private one-on-one instruction in order to get through troublesome areas of understanding or application.

a hands-on and ski-through experience

23

Coached Not Taught

Taos Ski Valley Super Ski Week receives a greater than average share of advanced skiers, who want to be coached not taught. They will watch and mimic great technique artfully demonstrated by the instructor, but quickly disregard preaching that is not applied. For the coach, the challenge is to understand the concept, apply it to themselves, and demonstrate it to the students while they explain it convincingly to help everyone apply the message.

Racing Speeds Understanding

Another unique learning approach at Taos is the use of racing both as an inspirational and instructional tool. This

> **understand the ski skills deeper and be able to apply them**

philosophy asserts that observation of the top ski racers of the world discloses the techniques proven successful in the most demanding arena of world class competition. When these leading-edge ideas are practiced through racing as a learning experience, you will understand the ski skills deeper and be able to apply them to a wider range of situations.

24

The Ultimate Teacher Is The Mountain

If you embrace the fundamental principle that the ultimate teacher is the mountain, the corollary is that instructors can fulfill their mission successfully by acting as guides. During Ski Week the term "instructor" is rarely used, but rather freely substituted with "coach" and "guide" as the focus changes from techniques, philosophy and drills to the terrain, snow and conditions on the mountain. The students learn from the mountain what is working and what is not.

When you ski the challenging terrain of Taos — its steeps, moguls, trees and non-groomed — it will give you feedback through your skis. You'll get messages like, "I'm fighting this too much" or "It's not biting enough." The coach's goal is to help you dance on the mountain, starting with the attitude of being in tune with what is happening between your skis and the snow.

by exposing the deficiency and motivating you to correct it now

It is also convenient to use the mountain as a teacher and a motivator. Perhaps you are pivoting excessively in the snow; the coaches will then lead you into a snow condition that will make it tough to do that. You then become very clear why that is not working and why it is important to use a different technique. The mountain helps you improve by exposing the deficiency and motivating you to correct it now. You have the challenge of improving your style to match the mountain.

A chute is another great classroom, for there is nothing more challenging than a narrow chute. Your first time down the chutes will make a believer out of you; if there is even a small problem, it will be dramatically emphasized.

25

New Mind-set

Skiing is now as natural as walking because of the new equipment. In walking, your feet are normally at shoulder width apart, your balance is centered, and your legs bend naturally. Walking can't be comfortably done with your ankles bound together or in any other convoluted positions. In skiing now, any turn or change of direction is also as natural as looking where you want to go and moving in that direction.

When guests enroll into a Ski Week program two things happen: their skiing ability improves and their love for skiing increases. Skiing-ability improvement comes from the challenge of Taos terrain and the unparalleled approach to the process of learning. Both generate, as a by-product, **a love of skiing and a passion for the mountain** which is so remarkable, it is almost an enhancement to their overall quality of life and a new mind-set. This is not merely learning how to turn left or right better. It truly is skiing as an art form.

By Jove,
I think you've got it.

"It's kind of weird, you know."

"What do you mean?" The wind was howling as we came up the lift over the top of Al's Run.

"I never saw you before we started this Ski Week, and now I feel like I've known you all my life. I think it is absolutely amazing," Chuck was more pensive than he had been all week.

"You're backsliding into your professional mode, I can see it clearly now." I whacked some snow off his ski with my pole, "I thought professors of psychology knew, better than anyone, how to unplug when they finally got away from it all."

"I do. I did," he stammered. "I can't believe what this week has been able to do for me. I can't remember the last time I was able to leave it all behind, and forget it all so completely."

We reached the top of Lift 1 and slid easily off the chair onto the snow and adjusted the straps on our poles, "Where do you want to go now?"

"To the top, to the trees, to the steeps," he faked a great French accent to mimic Jean Mayer, who not only was our host at the St. Bernard all week, but also did a couple of impromptu guest appearances in the Ski Week agenda. With that he started to pick up speed toward the base of Lift 2.

As we glided down the trail, I couldn't help but notice what a change had taken place in Chuck's style. He morphed from a hesitant stiff from California to a real skier, effortless in his movements, actually gaining speed on every turn as he carved his way down the hill, and finally relaxed. In less than a minute or so I was easing onto the chair, "No lift lines, don't you just love it?"

"It's got to be the intensity of the experience," he couldn't get off his analysis routine. I bet he was a gas in front of his students, "All we have been doing is skiing. And skiing like we have never skied before. I've been coming here for six years, and I've skied runs this week that I didn't even know existed."

I looked up at the beautiful West Basin Ridge. "You're getting such a kick out of this because you are a social animal, doing what you love to do, with other people, who are also doing what they love to do. Or like we say in Texas, we're all skiing our butts off, having a big ole' time," I concluded in my best Texan drawl.

"By Jove, I think you've got it," he shifted into his best, Richard Harris, English accent, direct from My Fair Lady, "we are all doing what we love to do, and we are focused while we do it. This living completely in the moment removes us from our past and binds us to the present, and binds us to all those sharing that event with us. It is camaraderie, par excellence."

Just then we got to the top of the lift, "Yeah, and you're happy because you think you are." I led the way toward the trees at the top of Pollux and looked back, "but you're right. This is great fun."

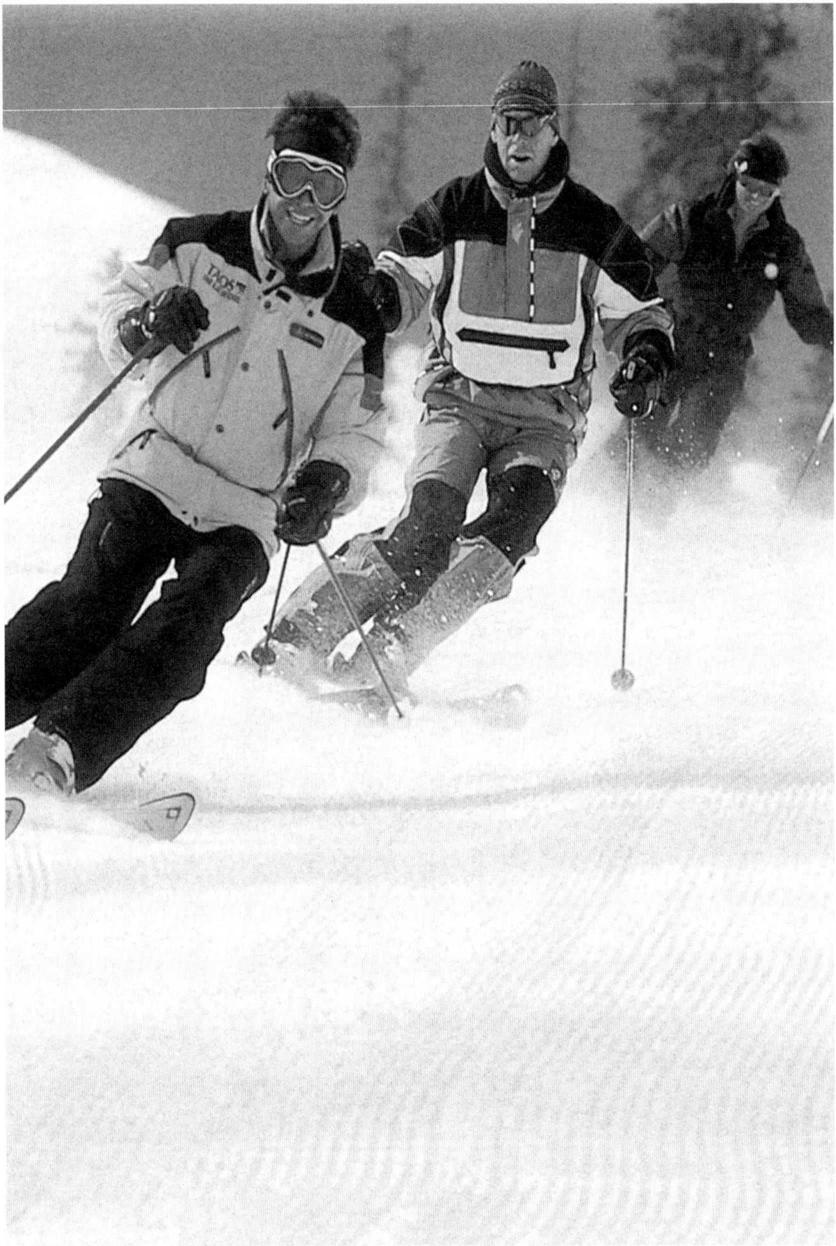

Fifth Run:

The Technical

Combines the physical, the mental and the emotional.

. . . don't miss the emotional while absorbed in the technical.

. . . tip the skis to turn, ski by design.

. . . find your center and your balance.

. . . still include grounding, centering, turning, body awareness, intensity, muscle involvement, position.

. . . have fun and respect the mountain.

. . . feel the snow, the slope, and go for it.

26

The Emotional Charge

Traditionally when you learn to ski, there is a major focus on the physical side of it, and rightly so. Better instructors and better ski schools also discuss the mental aspect of it, the learning mind frame, recognizing the anxiety and ego involvement.

Taos is unique in its recognition and use of the emotional charge of skiing as an integral part of its ski philosophy. It is important not to miss out on the emotional benefit of skiing while being absorbed in the technical. At the end of the day how many turns you did perfectly is not as important as how much you enjoyed the experience with the mountain and the environment.

The part of the Taos experience that makes a difference is learning to appreciate the surroundings and the magic of the moment.

> **how much you enjoyed the experience**

27

The Ruts of the Intermediate

Some of the most common problems for intermediate skiers sound like this, "I can do all the blues, but I just fall apart in the bumps . . . or when I get into the powder, I forget how to ski." If you are an intermediate, you may be a victim of the latest industry technology because advanced snow-grooming equipment and the summer improvements have leveled the playing field to allow you to do whatever you want on the groomed slopes. You can pivot, twist, skid or carve and get away with almost anything. However, it is the less than perfect conditions on the bumps, the powder, the steeps or in adventure areas that confront you with the painful evidence of bad habits, or lack of skill and confidence. Then the realization occurs that maybe something is missing in your skiing.

Turning is one of the most frequent targets for improvement, made more pervasive because it is a natural, instinctive movement. The instinct to turn relates to the skier's problem of trust in their skis which are designed to turn. Paradoxically, if you disabled the ski brakes on your skis, they would go straight down the hill. Skis need the appropriate signal in order to make the turns they are designed to make. That is why your whole focus in turning should be to give that ski the appropriate signal. At Taos, they tip or tilt the ski in order to give it the signal to go in the direction chosen. Imagine a plane that banks with its wings in order to change direction. As you ski, you actually have two planes flying in close formation: both have to bank simultaneously and in harmony in order to turn successfully.

tip the skis, trust them to turn, and ski by design

The trick in turning is not to balance on only the bottom of your feet, but to balance on the sides of your feet as well. The new shaped skis are shorter, softer and easier to carve than ever before.

Jean Mayer puts it this way:

"Both skis are edged the same and are parallel. However, it is very important to emphasize a strong alignment of the inside ski, which will allow in turn, the correct pressure with the outside ski."

"We work both skis, and to do so we need to incorporate a new modern move of the feet: a strong, lateral torquing of the feet, ankle sideways, and then of course the knee and maybe hip into the turn. You feel it in your ankle and your stomach muscles!"

This is the cornerstone of the Taos technique: be willing to tip the skis, trust them to turn, and ski by design.

28

Alignment, Alignment, Alignment

Alignment relates directly to the new boot technology because the feet are the initial receptacles of feedback from the hill and the implementors of commands from the body. What you feel in your feet is transmitted to your control system and executed by your skis. Instructors should identify any ill-fitting and outdated equipment, skis or boots that might keep you from experiencing the best you can be in skiing.

Alignment starts with supporting the foot in a stable position. Since about 80 percent of the population pronate their feet, some stabilizing of the arch is necessary in order to ensure that knee travel is aligned with the foot. A footbed is usually needed to achieve this stability. Actually, the center of the knee mass should travel fore and aft in a line between the big toe and the second toe to be in proper alignment and allow the skier to engage the edge of the ski into a turn. You can't have one without the other.

feel what is happening in your ski boot

Since you ski from your feet up, your sensors on the ground – your toes, arches, heels and ankles – must feel what is happening in your ski boot, to be able to translate the message to your knees, hips, shoulders and your brain. Each of these control points will in turn compensate for what its predecessor in the body's movement chain does not receive properly. The end result is a mess. Without proper alignment, you will search continually for your center and your balance, thus squandering the effortless motion possible in skiing.

29

The Fundamentals

The good news is that the fundamental principles haven't changed, only the equipment has. There are far more subtleties to enjoy.

Grounding.

You now need less power to ground yourself properly. It is more of a subtle, balanced stance because the skis are shorter and more shaped. Simply defined, grounding is finding yourself in total contact with the shape of the slope and the condition of the snow. This will allow you to sense your connection with the earth from your feet and extended throughout your body. Now with the new equipment, you need less muscular effort to make this happen.

Grounding gives you the body-mind awareness that is so essential to good skiing. This is also accelerated with the new equipment because you need less muscular effort in order to achieve this body-mind connection.

Centering.

Centering involves finding your sense of balance, your best and most efficient stance to achieve body alignment with muscles and skeleton. It is a relaxed stance, far less intense. The new equipment is much more responsive, providing much more life and spring to all of your movements.

a relaxed stance

Turning.

Basic to skiing is your ability to change direction in a controlled manner. The new equipment enhances your ability to change direction more easily because the essential shape of the ski is designed to turn. Your comfort increases dramatically.

Both skis are tilted on edge.

Jean Mayer describes it specifically: "For turning action, the lower body swings out from side to side, the head or chest balancing as the top of a pendulum. Both skis are tilted on edge and the driving force is exerted to initiate with the tips as the control is worked with the whole ski.

"The steeper the terrain, the more pressure is applied to the outside ski. The inside ski slightly leads the outside ski, the hips move forward to ensure power to the legs, all the way to the feet and the edge of the skis."

Body awareness.

Body awareness is close to centering as a concept yet maintains the distinction of a focus on totality. It is the sphere of total awareness from head to feet in the kinesthetic sense. Certainly some people have difficulty in differentiating between right and left, but more importantly, the major problem is fear of the unknown. Now the new equipment comes to the rescue through its basic design that favors turning and control, which is the key ingredient to reducing anxiety and fear in skiing. Seniors or people with disabilities can now attempt and succeed on terrain that they only dreamed of in the past: the powder, steeps or trees.

> **from head to feet**

Intensity.

Your concentration in skiing is really a matter of attitude that challenges yourself against the elements within reason and with respect. This challenge allows you to grow and learn more. It takes commitment to the moment to spawn intensity, but its reward is the relaxation of stress from your normal life. Why? When you ski

> **think about skiing and nothing but skiing**

you must think about skiing and nothing but skiing. Period. The intensity of your focus leverages the amount of tension release, in almost mathematical proportions. As your tension releases, your fun increases.

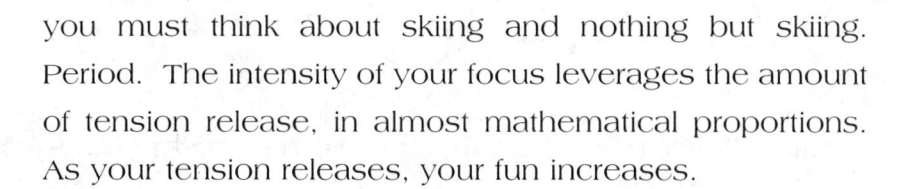

Muscle involvement.

The ability of your body to respond to the directives and whims of your mind is a fundamental necessity in skiing. Your muscles need to be in shape and prepared for the occasion. Being out of tune will get you too tired, too quickly. Better prepared muscles through training are also less stressed because they are relaxed more of the time.

Position.

Since the ideal skiing stance is now more erect with the new shorter skis, your position is more neutral, with less fore and aft movement, but considerably more lateral travel. Your upper body will lean farther away from your feet, very similar to surfing or any kind of gliding, which is more fun because you are defying gravity.

30

Jean's Important Points To Improve Ski Skills

Each year Jean Mayer provides a review of his current ski philosophy and technique to the instructors of Taos Ski Valley. Here is a recap of some of those important points to improve your ski skills:

- Establish a good sense of balance over the length of the skis.
- Your grounding and centering starts from the snow up.
- Even out the flexions of your ankles, knees and hips for good personal balance.
- If your fore, aft and lateral body movements are centered, they will enhance areas of support and pressure.
- Since skis are so short, you should start forward on your skis, and finish on the middle of them, centered.
- Maintain your feel of "touch" with pressure and release of pressure on the snow – weighting and unweighting.
- Proper alignment of your body will help you carry the forces and pressure over your skis.

- Weight distribution is now about 60% on the outside ski, but with more pressure carried on the inside ski than in the past.
- Proper pressure used in tipping your feet will help control carving.
- Develop lower body movement that allows your legs, feet and skis to move from side to side while your upper body stays quiet.
- Be aware and control your edge sets and their positions by properly tilting and tipping your feet and legs.
- Proper timing and flexibility of vertical leg actions will affect your movements from the snow.
- Be totally committed to your moves.
- When you ski the trees, bumps or crowds, look for the space between them.
- Use the latest ski equipment, it is designed to facilitate and improve your performance.
- Always have fun and be happy and respect the mountain.

Jean Mayer encourages you, "Never be afraid to test, challenge, or even return to the old styles, longer skis, and to the roots of where it all started."

always have fun and be happy

31

Attitude

Feel the snow. Feel the slope. Use them to enhance your moves while you blend your skills and your desire for fun. You can't be too shy, nor too reserved; if you seek a total experience of skiing, you'll have to work for it. Unfortunately, you cannot be defensive all the times because you will always be a step behind, or totally reactive. So within reason, don't hesitate — go for it!

don't hesitate — go for it!

The other aspect of a healthy attitude is the fun of it all. Don't get too wrapped up in trying to accomplish too much; remember that it is the process that is important. Gliding down the side of a mountain is an incredible adventure — enjoy it!

The Ridge

If you are on one of the groomed runs in Taos Ski Valley and look up the hill, the top of the mountain that touches the sky and rims the entire ski area is called THE Ridge. Not only is it the highest topographical feature, it is the mother lode of advanced and real expert ski experience at Taos.

Top of Chair 2 to the radio shack on THE Ridge is 300 vertical feet and about 320 yards.

Top of Chair 2 to Kachina Peak is 662 vertical feet, about one mile straight line, and just under 1.5 miles of walking distance.

Number of people who ski the Peak in an average season is slightly over 2,100. In the mid-70's, fewer people skied it in an entire season than now ski it in a single day.

Number of runs from THE Ridge is 96: 51 from West Basin, 33 from Highline, and 12 from Kachina.

Who named the chutes? Ernie Blake and The Ski Patrol.

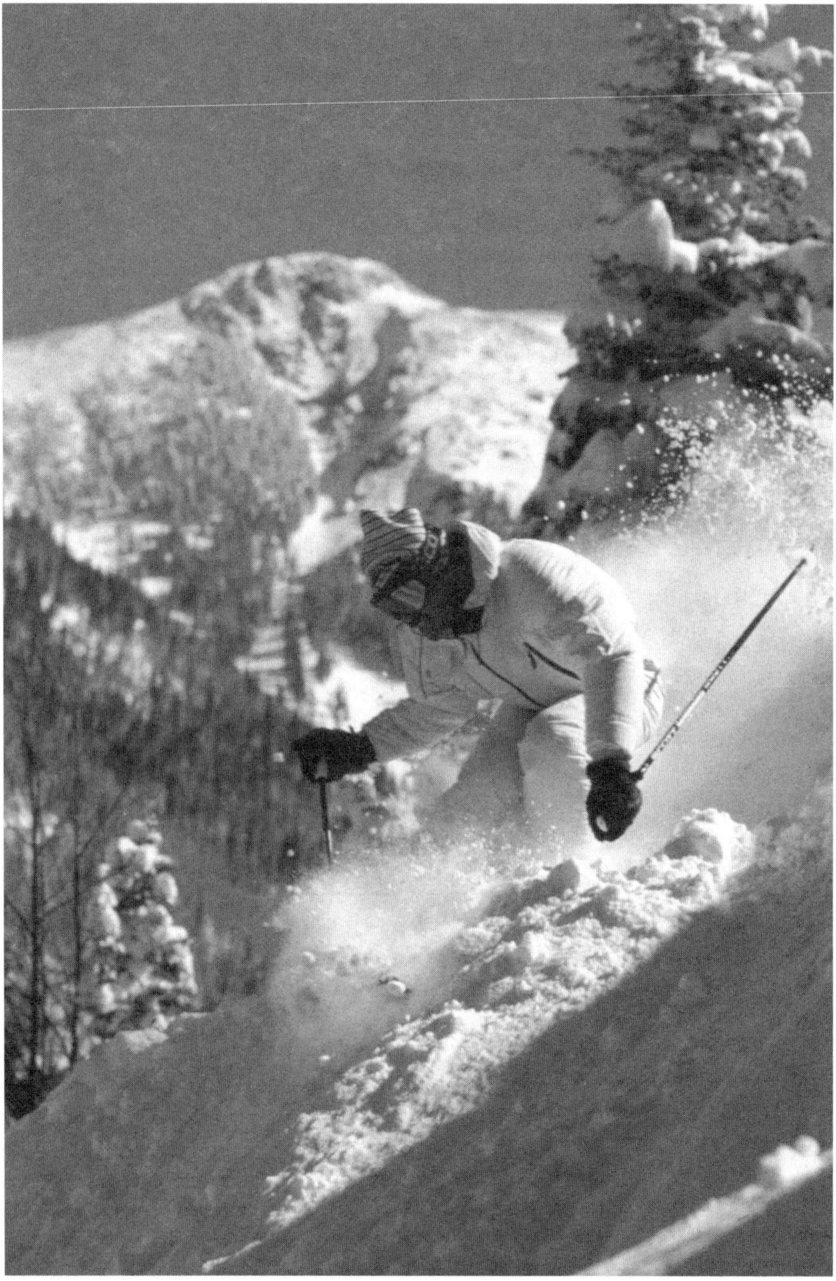

Sixth Run:

Bump Masters

Confidence dictates the activity.

. . . edge first to control the turn, then guide to get the result.

. . . if the leg locks, the skis run away.

. . . good technique plus knowing where to turn.

. . . the completion of one is the beginning of another.

. . . and release the pressure to start the turn.

. . . shape the turn on the top of the bump and guide it to the base.

. . . be natural for balance and make your turns.

. . . sometimes skiing is more tactical than technical.

Skiing in the bumps is a different and exciting part of skiing. In the bumps, you'll see the most variety in ski terrain as well as the most variety in technical approaches to skiing. The World Cup mogul skiers race down the hill on what they call the "zipper line," named because of its resemblance to a zipper laid on the mountain. Advance skiers look at the bumps and see all the changes of terrain as a great game field to jump, to twist and to bounce on as the mountain becomes a game board. Others will go to the bumps for the sheer challenge.

Whatever the approach, two items stay the same: confidence dictates the activity of the skier, and the release of the ski dictates the turn. From a technical point of view, the release of the edge is physically easier in the bumps than anywhere else on the mountain, and the release of the edge is the activity that will dominate the rest of the turn.

Much of this discussion is derived from Doug DeCoursey's approach to the bumps. Doug emphasizes a technique that allows a confident skier to master the terrain and provides an option to the more timid skier for skiing bumps on moderate terrain.

Again, confidence dictates your technique.

32

Edge First

In order to master the moguls, a skier should put the ski on edge first to control the turn, then guide or add more pressure to get the desired result. The new skis make this so much easier than ever before. No longer is there a requirement to change skis in order to do the bumps; it is fairly easy with the new equipment to find a single pair of skis that will do everything.

The problem that most skiers have in the bumps is controlling their speed. It was the original way bumps were taught that produced this problem: "plant the pole, come up, flatten the ski, twist it, tip into the fall line, then pressure and edge into the arc." If you did that, it would work in the moguls, and on ungroomed slopes. The human body figured out a way to control the skidding and sliding. In the past, that technique worked with the equipment available — you had to follow that sequence of movements or you couldn't turn.

edge first to get control then guide to get the result

Now the new equipment is physically easier to turn

because you move into the turn, which allows you to edge first, then guide the ski. This shapes the turn at the top prior to the fall line and is the biggest reason why moguls are easier than ever. Edge first doesn't mean a lot of edge angle; it means the movement of release to get the body on the new side.

A potent analogy is making a turn in a car on an icy road. When a turn is properly initiated, the wheel grips the surface of the road to change direction of the front end of the car, and the rear follows. However, when a turn is attempted in that same car with too much twisting, the rear end slides out of control.

In skiing, the older ski design was more difficult to edge into the top of the turn, unless you forced it. If you tried to tip it first, the old ski went straight and you fell down. The new equipment lets you successfully negotiate the bumps because it has a design that wants to turn.

33

Bend Your Knees, Watch Out For The Trees

One of the problems that most ski instructors address is their students' unwillingness to bend their knees in the bumps. The stiffening of the outside leg is usually caused by the idea of twisting the ski at the top of the turn, or a fear of the terrain; both have the same result. The leg locks, the ski runs away, and you are unable to finish the turn or control the ski. Thus the old mantra made sense because if you didn't bend your knees, the only thing to stop you was the trees.

> **the leg locks, the ski runs away**

Most people become masters at masking the stiff leg on nicely groomed snow, where they are more comfortable and can get away with anything. Many people, who consider themselves good skiers, say, "I ski great until the snow is thick, or junky, or moguls, or powdery, or whatever isn't groomed." The reality is that bumps or any adventure skiing conditions just expose those errors and impose a much greater penalty for poor technique.

34

Bumps Are All About Options

Some students must redirect their approach to the bumps to answer the statement " . . . if I just knew where to go I'd be all right." They think they are not mentally sharp enough for the bumps, but their technique will work. Yet it is really the other way around, because it is their technique that limits their ability to have options or choices in the bumps.

The bottom line to bump skiing is having options. Your body is brilliant at selecting an appropriate option. If you have only one technique from the "push, hit and hope school," the idea of pivoting the ski heavily and then finding the edge, makes it impossible to be the master of your destiny through the bumps. Even if you know where to turn, if you have bad technique, you won't be able to do it.

> **if you have bad technique, you won't be able to**

35

The Next Pole Plant

In bumps, the pole plant tends to be early. If you use a long flowing, giant slalom type of pole plant, you will get nothing but giant slalom types of turns which won't control your speed in the bumps. So a blocking pole plant, which allows the change of edges, tends to be early and is not a part of everyone's repertoire.

You should shape your turn with an edge angle and then guide it through rather than twisting, sliding or forcing it. It is a classic shaped turn where the tail goes through the same snow the tip went through. Instead of pivoting or displacing off of an axis to push and skid, it is the idea of tipping and riding through a path. The tightness of the turn will affect how much, or little, pivoting there will be in a turn. There are times when you need to make a very tight turn — to stay on a desired line, for a better route through the trees, or to control your speed. But this type of turn should be the exception, rather than the norm. Whenever possible, and for the best long-term approach to the bumps, keep the quality of your turns high by using this tip, then guide the approach.

At the completion of every successful pole plant is the

beginning of the next pole plant and preparation for the next turn. The moment one pole plant is done, is the moment the next pole plant starts. Whether you choose to turn there or not, you must be ready.

keeps the body quiet and balanced

The next pole plant is what separates the experts, who keep their bodies straight down the hill, from those who throw themselves down the fall line and end up going across the slope. Just take a second to analyze any fantastic bump skier and you'll see a quiet, relaxed upper body in which one pole plant leads inexorably to the next. The second pole plant also keeps the body quiet and balanced in preparation for the next turn. This keeps the upper body down the hill and allows the legs to finish the turn.

36

Release The Edge

Success in the bumps also leads to the question of how to start the turn. The start of each turn is restricted by the edge and pressure on the edge of the previous turn. So, the release of the edge, and hence the pressure, is imperative to start a turn.

In all forms of skiing, especially in the bumps on contemporary equipment, the edge release starts at the bottom of your foot — the sole of skiing. It is the lateral tipping of the feet that starts the turn and dictates where the body will move. You can move your head and eventually your feet will follow, but you want your feet to roll so that your body will move into the direction of the new turn.

Just remember it's the feet that release you, and the body, into the turn.

starts at the bottom of your foot

37

S Not Z

If you want a line to ski the bumps, simply come to the top of the bump with the tips hanging over, begin shaping the turn on the top and guide it around the base of the bump.

As you are doing this, if you can't handle the speed, cut it in half and put two turns per bump, always making arcs or "S" turns rather than "Z" turns.

always making arcs

It is edge control throughout the turn.

38

A Different Focus
– Weighting, Balance and Absorption

Since you tend to be more simultaneous in your movements now, you no longer talk about the term "weight transfer." When you analyze it, there is more weight on the outside ski, not because you put it there, but because inertia will naturally affect it more there. So undue attention to weight transfer will usually create the old approach to the bumps as in the mantra, "plant the pole, come up, flatten the ski, twist it, tip into the fall line, then pressure and edge into the arc." Try to maintain a natural stance at all cost.

Balance is a term that is used carefully because the body naturally strives to achieve balance. Your balance is derived from your appropriate movements which dictate the shape of your turns, control and ultimate comfort.

The last aspect in any mogul discussion is the popular belief that the real key to skiing moguls is absorption. In reality, minimizing absorption is the right attitude, so use it judiciously to keep from punishing your body, not as a mind-set. Go back to our basic discussion to realize that if your thought coming into a bump is to compress as the bump comes up and stretch as the bump goes down, you tend not to turn. Since the ski remains fairly flat when you do want to slow down, it tends to be a twist-and-push thing.

try to maintain a natural stance

39

Something You Don't Have To Do

Moguls are changes in terrain caused by skiers, some good and some bad. Those moguls created by good skiers can be a rewarding experience where you can apply a sense of balance, rhythm and technique. However, those moguls created by poor skiers might require more athleticism and almost a defensive attitude from you in order to navigate them successfully. Since you assess these conditions while you are in the moguls, your skiing then becomes more tactical rather than technical. Wisdom, common sense, good judgment, choice, options, your ability . . . all should be considered as you approach the mogul run.

some moguls are an insult

Remember, moguls are something you don't have to do. Too many people attack moguls as if they were the ultimate grade on their skiing abilities. Realistically we must remind that crowd that some moguls are an insult to our intelligence, created by poor skiers who jump around haphazardly or traverse the hill. Sure you can get down the hill, but the joy of a good mogul is lost, simply replaced by the accomplishment of surviving the slope.

Trail Names

Earliest Runs on the Lower Front

Al's Run: Named for Al Rosen, the famous Taos surgeon politically instrumental in getting the Ski Valley off the ground. He skied with an oxygen mask and tank for twenty years until his death in 1982.

Edelweiss: The edelweiss is the hard-to-get flower of the Alps; it is the distinctive flower all over the Alps. It also represents first life or rebirth.

Firlefanz: "Firlefanz" is a German term for something extra, like silver threads on a Christmas tree.

Hannes Schneider: Hannes came to the USA in December of 1938, after having been arrested by the Germans after they took over Austria. Harvey Gibson, a New York banker, bought Schneider's freedom and brought him to North Conway, New Hampshire to organize a ski school. He invented the Learn to Ski Week.

Inferno: Named after the famous race started by the Ski Club of Great Britain and the Kandahar Club in Murren, Switzerland. It is an old race, and one of the longest, most vertically difficult runs in the world.

Jean's Glade: Named for Jean Mayer, Technical Director of Taos Ski Valley Ski School and owner of the St. Bernard Hotel.

Longhorn: A slang reference for a Texan and a rare breed of cattle having long horns. First run from the top of the mountain.

Porcupine: An animal with stiff, sharp, erectile bristles.

Powderhorn: A flask for carrying gunpowder.

Psycho Path: A path for "psychos." Named by Wolfie Lert.

Rhonda's Revenge: Rhonda Blake had found this little cut off so she didn't have to ski the first steep part of Al's Run.

Showdown: An army term, or gunfighter term.

Snakedance: Named by Wolfie Lert for the Hopi dancers.

Spencer's Bowl: For E.J. Spencer, Ernie Blake's favorite English teacher and coach from his school in Engadine, Switzerland.

Strawberry Hill: Is the beginner's run with lots of strawberries in the summer.

Tell Glade: Named for William Tell, the crossbow-shooting marksman, who is also the liberating Swiss hero of the Rossini/Schiller opera.

White Feather: An easy path. In England, gentlemen who didn't volunteer for the army in the Boer War were sent white feathers, the symbol of cowards, by their girl acquaintances. This name typifies Ernie Blake's wry sense of humor and ironic wit.

Runs From the Top

Bambi: "Bambi" from the Disney movie of the same name.

Blitz: This is the German term for lightning.

Bonanza: An exceptionally large vein of gold or silver.

Castor and Pollux: These twins of Greek and Roman mythology gave their names to the bright stars in the constellation Gemini.

Honeysuckle: Named for the lovely and fragrant flower.

Lorelei: "Lorelei" is the German Siren; it is like a beautiful woman who is very admired but who is dangerous. On the run, there's a giant rock field on the right with narrow paths likened to a woman's figure.

Reforma: Reforma refers to the Mexico City boulevard that honors Benito Juarez and the Mexican Revolution.

Sir Arnold Lunn: A British skier largely responsible for making skiing a competitive sport and who set the first slalom course in 1922. Through his efforts, slalom skiing was recognized in the 1936 Olympics.

Werner Chute: For Werner Duettra, caught in a slide in 1971.

Winston: A double black diamond named for the World War II Prime Minister of Britain.

Zagava: John Zagava was one of the partners in the original Hondo Lodge in 1946.

Backside – Kachina Basin

El Funko: Named for a local businessman who was not an especially gifted skier and may well have fainted at his first sight of this cliff-like run.

Hunziker Bowl: Ernie Blake's favorite run, which will never have a lift. Named for Paul Hunziker, the Swiss engineer who designed the first Kachina lift.

Japanese Flag: One of the many flags at the Ski Valley; this one used to survey the Kachina lift area.

Kachina Basin: Named for one of the deified ancestral spirits to visit the pueblos at intervals, according to the Hopi and other Pueblo Indian legends.

Lone Star: Named in honor of the Texas flag.

Maxie's: For the great New Mexican balloonist, Maxie Anderson, who made the first Atlantic crossing in a balloon.

Papa and Baby Bear: Two of three original trails on the Kachina Basin.

Patton: "Patton" is named in honor of a remarkable commanding general, George Patton. He was one of the greatest American leaders of World War II.

Rubezahl: Rubezahl is a red-haired, one-eyed East German mythological giant who takes money from the rich and gives it to the poor. The first and longest run down the backside of the mountain.

Shalako: Named for Indian dancers celebrating a Zuni mystical being of extraordinary stature.

Totemoff: "Totemoff" is named after Pete Totemoff, an Aleut Indian from Alaska. He and Ernie Blake first looked at Taos Ski Valley from the air and on the ground.

Walkyries: From Norse mythology. The Walkyries were the wood nymphs who tended the battleslain warriors and led them to Norse heaven – Valhalla.

Winkelried: A Swiss patriot who led farmers with no breastplates, just knives and axes in 1386 to fight the Austrian army.

The Ridge

Fabian: "Fabian" was named for Fabian von Schlaberndorff, a technician, who unsuccessfully plotted to kill Hitler. In 1946, he wrote a book, They Almost Killed Hitler.

Hidalgo: Named for the Mexican martyr and patriot-priest who perished in his attempt to bring about Mexican Independence in 1810.

Juarez: The notably honest and gifted pure-blooded Indian who brought justice and recognition to the Indians and mixed-blood populations of Mexico.

Niňos Heroes: Young Mexican cadets who all died in defense of Chapultepec Castle during the Mexican-American conflict of 1846.

Oster: "Oster" was a German general, in the German Military Intelligence Service. He sabotaged the German war effort and was executed by Hitler's men.

Spitfire: Named for the British World War II fighter plane.

Stauffenberg: "Stauffenberg" was the general who successfully placed a bomb in Hitler's bunker, but unfortunately missed Hitler.

Tresckow: Another supreme patriot who conspired to eliminate Hitler.

Zdarsky: The Austrian engineer, Mathias Zdarsky, born in 1856, who wrote the first really useful ski manual in 1897.

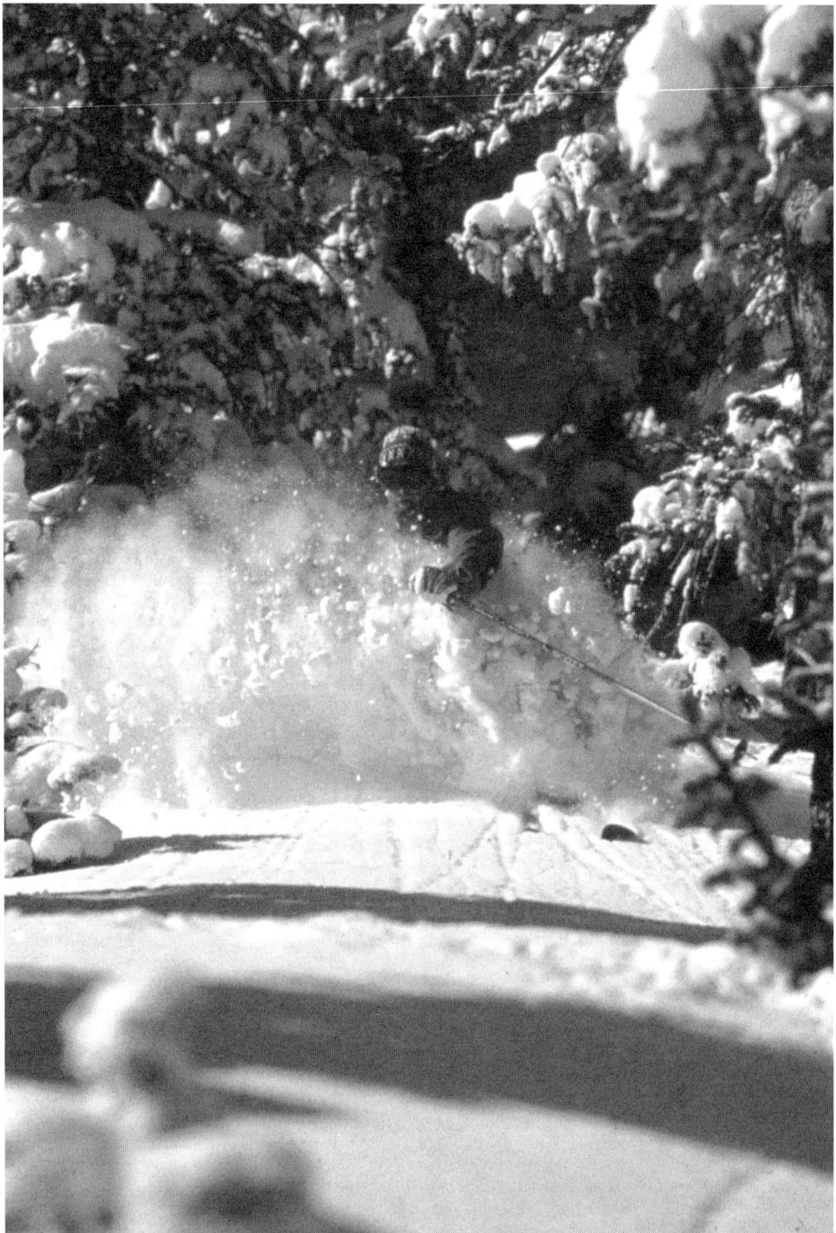

Seventh Run:

Adventure Skiing

The everlasting search for fresh, untracked powder and soul.

. . . observe a back-country attitude and your own limitations.

. . . if the tip deviates, you will meet resistance.

. . . don't lean too far back in powder — use the ski as a tool.

. . . be perpendicular, be centered.

. . . transition effortlessly between conditions.

. . . have fun in gullies, look for spaces, watch your landings.

. . . add versatility with a jump, kick and a traverse.

. . . shape your turn or you'll be penalized.

. . . the secret in powder is to trust the new equipment.

. . . the character of the terrain adds more fun.

40

Adventure Skiing Is Self-Reliance

Adventure skiing is a common reference for skiing off the packed snow, whatever that may be. People like to ski off the groomed runs for the adventure and the everlasting search for fresh, untracked powder, which does strange things to one's soul. It is the softness and slowness of it, the feeling of self-reliance and achievement, the joy of a slope without other people. In Taos you may find adventure skiing when you venture off a blue run, in the form of steeps, trees, chutes or the deep.

Never Turn Off Your Brain

At Taos Ski Valley, the ski area is defined and surrounded by the Wheeler Wilderness, as established by Congress in 1963. The premise of the wilderness area is that access is permitted only under your own (non-mechanical) power. Since the chairlift is a mechanical device, if you access the wilderness from it, you technically are in violation of the Act. "No room to grow" is also one of the major factors that has kept Taos the way it is, without major expansion options, nor massive real estate projects. TSV's objective has been to improve what is in their boundaries as opposed to expanding the terrain. As a result, they continue to increase their level of refinement compared to other ski areas.

Another limitation for TSV's adventure skiing is its rating as a Class A Avalanche Area, which is the highest hazard for avalanches. After one heavy snow period, Taos had 135 avalanches inbounds, in a period of five days. The ski patrol will close runs to manage the potential for avalanche hazards, which they take very seriously.

ski with a back-country attitude

By far the most important limitations are your own. Just because you can hike up the peak, doesn't mean you can ski down it. Unfortunately, some people get trapped in a Disneyland mentality that suggests a ski area is as controlled as a big amusement park, where things never go wrong and everything is completely safe. Consider the fact that if someone has a problem or mishap on Kachina Peak, it will take the Ski Patrol at least forty-five minutes to get to the person, once they receive notification. There are no helicopters awaiting to pluck you off a rock or out of a life-threatening situation, and you are at the mercy of your own devices.

When you are adventure skiing, ski with a backcountry attitude laced with a heightened awareness of snow conditions. If a run is open and patrolled, it doesn't mean that it is safe and it won't avalanche. You must consider safety at all times and never turn off your brain. When it comes to equipment, an avalanche beacon might save your life. Many of the locals will wear their transceivers on any powder day plus other basic survival equipment in their backpack on every hike up to Kachina Peak. This equipment is available at most mountaineering shops.

PHOTO TSV/Ken Gallard

PHOTO TSV/Ken Gallard

PHOTO TSV/Ken Gallard

PHOTO TSV/Ken Gallard

PHOTO TSV/Ken Gallard

PHOTO TSV/Ken Gallard

PHOTO TSV/Colin Samuels

PHOTO TSV/Ken Gallard

41

Break Trail For The Tail

The key issue in skiing non-groomed snow conditions is to make your tip break trail for the tail. Make the tip act like an icebreaker going through frozen waters, and break a path for the rest of your ski to follow. If your tip deviates, you will twist and torque your ski out of that path to meet resistance and find trouble.

The side wall of the ski is a very blunt part of your ski. If the side wall hits crust, porridge or crud, you will receive a very strong feedback that may make you go down. Here is where the training done on the groomed runs comes into play, because all the carving techniques are invaluable in any variable snow. You do not have to carve per se, but as long as your ski tip is creating a path for the rest of your ski to follow, you will find it much easier to travel in these conditions.

make the tip act like an icebreaker

During skiing on variable snow conditions, the idea of grounding and centering on your skis is extremely important. If you are too far forward in wind crust, or "just leaning back in the powder," you are headed for trouble. Rather, balance your weight over the center of the ski as you would on the groomed slopes. Challenging snow conditions are invaluable to demonstrate the value of good basic technique and how to take advantage of your ski's design as a tool.

42

The Powder And The Resistance

How do you ski the powder? First, remember the attraction of powder is simply the fun of powder. It is soft, it billows, it cushions, it flies out of your way as you leave a wake that floats in the air and leaves the signature of your creativity.

Of course, others will say that it is the resistance of the snow that slows you down to ski a steeper run with less effort and more confidence. This resistance doesn't allow you to accelerate like you would on hard pack, so the first thing you should do is to make sure that you have the right kind of skis. There is simply nothing to match the thrill of powder skis on a deep powder day!

Second, remember not to lean too far back when you feel the resistance of the snow. This tendency comes from one of the skier's biggest fears in the powder, an ostrich stop, or falling head first into the snow. To compensate for this, skiers lean all the way back to give themselves a cushion against those sudden stops. The correct technique is to keep your stomach muscles taut so

remember not to lean too far back

when your skis start to decelerate suddenly, instead of flopping over like a rag doll, your mid-body will keep the ski moving, leading the way and penetrating the snow. Be centered and be strong to penetrate the powder.

The Porpoise Turn

Adventure skiing demands that you maintain the appropriate speed control for the snow conditions. Deep powder might make it impossible to turn across the hill in order to slow down because you can't point the skis where you want to go. Instead, try turning like a porpoise: if you want to slow down, put your tips down into the snow, and the deeper they get the slower you go. To increase your speed, simply flatten your skis out again, and let them rise like a porpoise. To get the tips down again without a tremendous show of strength, just tip them to expose the side walls to the snow which will make them dip.

Sometimes speed is not the point. Sometimes it is the sheer enjoyment of coming in and out of the powder, letting your skis explode back into view like a submarine surfacing from the deep. Have fun.

The Jump Turn

In the narrow chutes, when there are wind-crust snow

conditions and little room for broad sweeping turns, consider the jump turn to change direction. This is not a good technique to use all the time but is totally a situation-dependent, survival move when a quick direction change is necessary. By jumping, you free your skis from the resistance of the snow and change directions in the air. Remember: this is a last option.

The Ski As A Tool

You shouldn't have to change technique when you ski the race course or the powder, other than some adjustments in balance and priorities. Use your ski as a tool. If you try to turn your ski while it is flat, it will slide around the turn and your balance will be difficult to maintain because there is no resistance in the snow. On the other hand, if you tilt the ski on its edge, you will put significant resistance into the snow and the ski will change direction. But the deep powder can also change this too, because the snow packing under the ski may create angles.

use the side cut, the bow and the shape of the ski to turn

This is the basic premise of all good skiing: use the side cut, the bow and the shape of the ski to do exactly what it is supposed to do, to turn. In the powder and the bumps, the softer skis will bow more and therefore turn more.

43

Move With The Mountain

In steeper terrain, maintain a perpendicular relationship with the hill. Be centered on your skis. If you are cruising down the cat walk, it is easy to be centered on your skis because your natural stance is perpendicular with the slope. In this instance, you are also vertical.

When skiing the steeps, perpendicular is no longer vertical. In order to stay in balance on the steeps, you need to move through a perpendicular attitude, and commit to movement down the hill — one of the biggest challenges of the steeps.

maintain a perpendicular relationship with the hill

One of the real accomplishments of the Ski Week program is its ability to help you feel the skis and to be in balance with the hill.

44

Timing Is Everything

If you are skiing properly, you can transition effortlessly from one snow condition to the next, whether it is powder, or crud, or crust, or whatever is there. That is one of the true definitions of an expert skier . . . one who can ski any snow condition, any time, at any speed. You can start a run at Kachina Peak in light powder and by the time you reach the bottom you may be in different, heavy conditions. Yet you don't need to change technique, only adjust pressure to preserve your angles, your radius of turning and your tactical approach.

Timing separates the great skier from all the rest. This distinction is important because you can make all the right moves at the wrong time and it won't do you any good. If you have good timing, you can ski from one snow condition to the next snow condition without a care.

don't make the right moves at the wrong time

Skiing in a variety of snow conditions is helpful to define your options. You learn what won't work, and conversely the options that are true. You should be able to ski from one condition to the other with no change of technique, because technique doesn't change — timing and tactics do.

45

Bite A Piece Of Freedom

Adventure skiing is biting a piece of freedom and trying to find a line where no one else has been; trying to dominate the slope without being intimidated by the mountain. The secret is riding the terrain, being as harmonious as possible, yet fast and confident, with the intent to dominate. Don't lull yourself into complacency; you will have to concentrate more, but the exhilaration is beyond compare.

Gullies Are Fun

Any kind of concave surface, whether it is a chute, ditch or the space in between two bumps, is a challenge because skis hang up tip to tail. Skis seem to grow in gullies; they can hang up on every branch or catch on every rock.

Do a turn in a gully or a chute or anywhere your tip and tail touch the vertical. Concave is a lot more difficult to ski than the convex, because the convex area of a ridge or top of a bump allows you stand in the middle of your skis, completely free to pivot in any direction. On the other hand, concave terrain amplifies everything when the ski tip and tail touch the upward sides of the gully, which allows you to bank off the surface like a wave or it can unforgivingly stop movement as your skis catch on the wall.

Gullies are a big danger in avalanche country, and they are always considered terrain traps. The snow can cascade down either side of the depression as well as from above to bury you, increasing the danger to three fronts.

The only way to conquer the gully is by an interesting blend of patience and aggression. Your attitude has to be very aggressive, "I want to go down the hill," yet you must be patient with your skis because they won't come around nearly as quickly as they would under normal conditions on a flat or a convex run.

Commonly the skier with the problem in the gully is one who reverses the paradigm and is aggressive with his skis and patient with his attitude about getting down the hill. This skier fights the hill by trying to turn the skis without losing any elevation. Very tough. No matter which herky-jerky movement is attempted, it is hard to overcome the resistance of gravity.

blend of patience and aggression

Look For Spaces Not Trees

The best advice for skiing in the trees is still the simplest: don't concentrate on the trees but focus on the way to go around them. Skiing anywhere has the same rules; you should look where you want to go and not at the obstacles. The hazards may be the trees, but the root problem is mental. If all you can see are trees, you will balk and unconsciously create a problem. It is easy to overlook the real difficulty with trees; this is usually the steepness of the hill, the unevenness of the terrain, or even the irregularity of the snow.

A Simple Commitment Move

When you consider skiing off a cornice, start off by checking it out thoroughly because most cornices require some sort of a jump, some sort of leaving the planet for a brief moment of time, followed by some sort of a landing. Hopefully, this will be the sort of a landing which was thought out.

if you didn't check out the landing, don't do the jump

The simplest rule prevails: if you didn't check out the landing, don't do the jump.

Once you have figured out where you are going to land, skiing the cornice is a simple jump. The cornice is not the edge of the earth, but it is the edge of the snow. Most problems occur when people peek over the edge of the snow, and it breaks off ten feet behind them as they become the latest avalanche down the hill.

46

A Bag Of Tricks

Being versatile is the key to enjoyment and survival in any adventure skiing environment.

A versatile tool for a change of direction is a jump turn, where you jump up, turn 180 degrees and then land. It is important to practice a jump turn on a steep groomed run under somewhat controlled conditions, rather than to do your experimentation in a chute — especially in a chute that is only as wide as your skis are long. No amount of strategizing, philosophizing or discussions will prepare you adequately for an athleticism required for a jump turn in a chute. Learn it on your own in class, but practice it until it is a reflexive action.

The second basic maneuver is the kick turn, one of the staple maneuvers of the 1930's if you wanted to get down any mountain. Start in a position perpendicular to the direction of the slope with no lateral movement. Pick up your downhill ski and turn it 180 degrees so that it is pointing in the opposite direction from your base ski, then turn the base ski 180 degrees to match it. The net result is a complete, safe, stationary change of direction, perfect for tight locations such as a chute, a gully or very steep terrain.

At Squaw Valley Resort, there is a famous run called KT22. The story goes that "KT" stands for "kick turn" and 22 represents the number of kick turns it took for the wife of the original owner to get down the hill.

Actually, with a good kick turn and a steady traverse, you can virtually ski anything that can be skied, but without them you may find yourself in trouble. A simple traverse allows you to negotiate a hill within your comfort range, no matter what your ability level.

be determined to get down the hill

For adventure skiing, the main consideration is controlling your skis and your path as well as maintaining that determination to ski down the hill. Nothing in our day-to-day life has prepared us for moving down the direction of the hill or sliding down the slope standing up. This spells job security, par excellence, for ski instructors.

If you want to ski better, be determined to get down the hill. If you fight it, you may fall into all the bad habits of fighting gravity. The best skiers don't fight gravity; they play with it. There is no substitute for developing your willingness to go down the hill, just lean into the fall line and go.

47

Shape Your Turn For Adventure Skiing

Will an ability to handle the bumps help in skiing in adventure areas? Sure. Of course, there is a change in the timing issue, movement patterns stretch out, and there is not the necessity to be quite as quick. The ultimate key, especially with the new equipment, is shaping the turn at the top. One of the penalties for twisting in the bumps is a Z-shaped turn where your skis run away and your balance erodes, putting you in the back seat consistently. Although bumps can make it easy to turn, in the powder of adventure skiing, you are again penalized heavily for trying to twist by the massive resistance of the snow.

The ultimate breakthrough in powder and crud skiing is gaining the confidence to deal with the speed that comes from skiing in these conditions. There is a real irony here. The snow is actually slowing you down, but the resistance of the snow also inhibits your ability to slip the ski, which is the real speed-reduction device. The best way to deal with this new sensation (not being able to scrub off speed by slipping) is to pick terrain with which you are confident in skiing, and which will allow you to be free and comfortable in a slightly different environment. Many skiers find the best place to become comfortable in powder is on a pitch with a flatter run out. Much like a runaway truck ramp, this terrain allows you to go for it with a bit of an escape route.

It is very helpful to have simultaneity of foot action to shape the turn at the top and use the ski design efficiently. You can cut crud as easily as you can cut powder. The start of the turn takes longer in powder and crud because of the increased resistance. When you're confident to be patient at the start of your turn in these conditions, you are well on your way to becoming a master of the deep.

the start of the turn takes longer

48

Equipment Helps

Equipment is a huge issue in adventure skiing. The new powder skis are awesome in their ability to improve your performance in the challenging conditions of thick or exceptionally deep powder. Nothing changes in powder of six to eight inches, so use your regular equipment. As the powder snow becomes heavier, the difficulty level increases exponentially. Touch, balance and finesse are real attributes of the powder skier, but the old dictum of adding more vertical motion no longer is applicable with the modern powder skis.

simply tip and balance on them and they turn

For average skiers, their experience level in powder is considerably less than in regular snow. These beginning powder skiers start out the run in a classic defensive mode of leaning back, stiffening their legs, holding their breath, and stopping all hope for success. The secret to skiing powder is to trust the new equipment. The more you use the vertical movement, the more you take away for the idea of moving from edge to edge. In other words, on old equipment, you had to unweight the skis in order to turn them; now you simply tip and balance on them and they turn. Crud and powder offer additional resistance, so you may have to help the process by augmenting the release.

49

Adventure Is More Rewarding

In adventure skiing, use the advantage of ski design and continue guiding the ski along its inside edge. We can write endlessly about skiing on the steep terrain and the different conditions that exist in Taos; however, these are a learned activity for experienced skiers. Can you imagine trying to learn how to swim out of a book, and then jumping into the deep end of a swimming pool? This information is to inspire and help you visualize how to improve your skiing. But, for the ultimate benefit, go to the mountain where you can be exposed to the thrill of advanced skiing.

At Taos Ski Valley, a lot of the mountain is adventure skiing because it is more creative. Just by the very nature of this terrain, the sense and spirit of the mountain, TSV endeavors to maintain the integrity of the slope and the autonomy of each run. This character adds more fun, more excitement and a deeper reward to your experience.

for the ultimate benefit, go to the mountain

I finally made it

"There hasn't been a mountain on the east coast that I haven't been to," thought Joe as he sat back in his seat aboard Southwest Flight 135 from Albuquerque to Newark. "I ate up those icy, crowded, old, cold, rugged hills, just to get a shot at skiing. And after twelve years of instructing, I finally made it out west. Man, what have I missed!"

The big bird gently rolled off the runway and climbed skyward to cruising altitude and turned away from Sandia Peak. Joe looked out the window, "Taos mountain was huge — it topped out at over 12,000 feet. Snow was so soft it felt like white air. After all those years on frozen hard pack, it was quite an adjustment to make from the hold-and-bite mentality I had with skis all those years to actually decreasing the pressure on the skis, allowing more flowing and gliding."

"With that smile on your face, I'd give a brand new bottle of wine to find out what you're dreaming about," said the flight attendant standing in the aisle.

He almost blushed, "It was a hoot." His smile broadened, "it was my first time."

Her smile really broadened to a chuckle.

"It was a hoot; it was almost like flying," he returned his silent gaze out the window, "I had more speed than I ever had and was amazed at how much distance and speed it required on my turns. But the most important thing was how relaxed I was; for the first time I didn't have a death grip on the hill; I just enjoyed the ride down."

As his eyes closed and his head nodded slowly, "I almost know what they mean when they say 'harmonize with the mountain'."

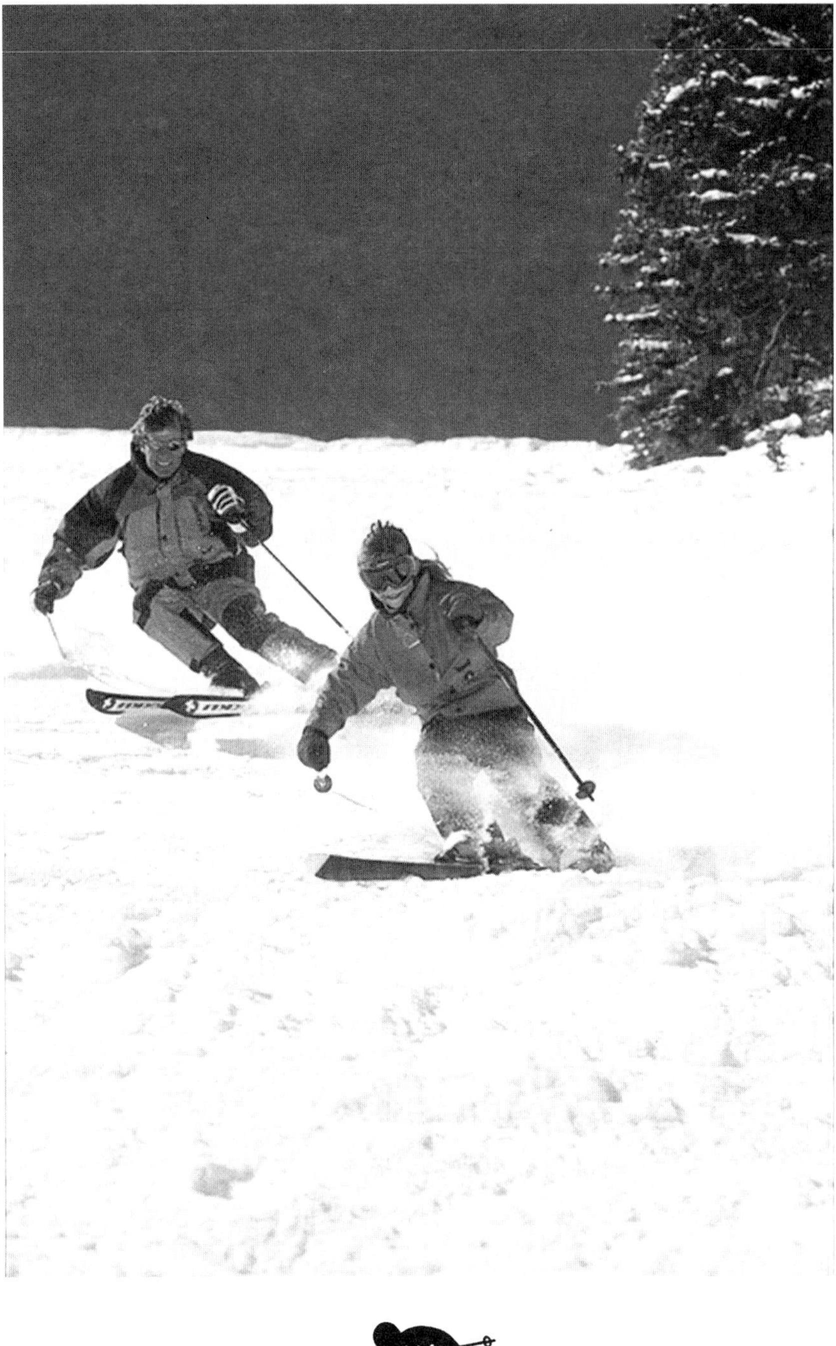

Eighth Run:

The Kids

A learning machine.

. . . a fun-oriented time that feels good.

. . . learning specifically designed for kids, with buy-in techniques that work.

. . . child centered and parent friendly to minimize separation anxiety.

. . . the keys are balance, flexibility and anticipation.

. . . trick children into learning.

. . . not coaching, but watching and imitating.

. . . active kids learn faster starting at an early age.

. . . good things take time.

50

For Children, Learning Must Be Fun

Children are amazing in their ability to learn. Start with agility and flexibility, natural curiosity, a penchant for emulation, then add a healthy dose of fearlessness, and you have the makings of a learning machine.

But only if they want to.

Children learn by example – by copying, mimicking and doing what you do – especially anything that is fun and exciting! You cannot tell children very much that will stick with them, but you can show them a lot. Since they are very keen on sensations, don't try to explain or analyze the technical; simply do a lot like catching air, exploring, or finding powder.

Always be careful that children are comfortable, not too hot nor too cold. Everything should be fun, so, in order to make them aware of the terrain, create a lot of games, organized around doing things that will drive home some skiing fundamentals. After all, you are in one of the most amazing amusement parks ever created in nature!

You should not place too many expectations on your

child. Basically, skiing is a fun-oriented time that feels good, and not necessarily a result-oriented task that is picture perfect. Anxieties and concerns frequently start early in a child's skiing career, traceable to the parents.

you cannot tell children very much

51

Center On Learning

Taos is also for the little people, centering on whatever it takes for children to learn, even going so far as to design the lifts especially to reduce their apprehension about this new activity. There is an effortless people mover and even the beginner's chairlift has a special, low profile to the snow, just right for the little ones.

There is a difference in ski instruction technique to children of various age levels, and Taos accommodates those differences in the Children's Learning Center. If it sounds basic it is, but it is also frequently overlooked by other areas.

learning is processed quite differently in early childhood

Learning is processed quite differently in early childhood — between the ages of three to first grade — not particularly verbal but with a good quotient of experimentation. Since there is also a lack of muscular development in this same age group, the child is supported more by the skeleton. Many times these youngsters balance back in their boot as well as being a little stiff legged.

Children do whatever it takes to stand up, so they tend to be more natural and appear to use the equipment differently. Sometimes this causes concern with the parents, "My children are sitting back on their skis; why are they stiff legged?" Since the child relies more on the skeletal frame than muscle, it is amazing they are able to stand up at all. So things that appear to be wrong, often are just right for the child — for now.

Just about the time the child gets to the first grade or about six years old, things change again. The directive approach using commands like, "put your foot out here" or "do that," is supplemented by the more "buy-in" techniques of teaching such as, "Who can stand like this?" and "Can you move like this?" The instructor sets up an environment where learning can occur versus a traditional teaching scenario.

52

Separate The Parents From The Kids

The Children's Center creates an atmosphere that it is completely child centered and parent friendly. For the parents, it is a one-stop and one-step shop where all the major hassles of rentals, fittings, and food are eliminated. Some forms must be filled out at the beginning of the process, but the good news is that the Children's Center takes over from there. Since they are totally self-contained, the staff takes care of fitting the boots, skis and poles and then entertains the children until the lesson begins. Children learn better in smaller classes where the group is homogeneous; for the three– to five–year olds, the class size is four or less; other children's classes are seven or less.

> **Peace of mind is assured**

Food is the last part of the equation, and lunch, snacks and water are provided for the children. Peace of mind is assured with well-qualified staff, but for those parents with special concerns, pagers are available to provide a direct connection throughout the day.

The bottom line is great for the parents and great for the

kids. Parents have more free time, less frustration and are secure in the knowledge that their children are in a happy, learning environment where all their needs are met.

Only Once

Psychologically and emotionally, the parents of the very young must be ready for possible separation anxiety if this ski school experience is their first time apart. Parents should separate only once, and give the separation a chance to work. If the child sees the parent again after the initial separation, it adds an additional layer of difficulty to the situation. Whether it is watching by the fence or skiing by to check out progress, the visible parental presence undermines that initial break and transfer of authority.

Children, especially small ones, like to have a clue as to what will happen during the day, so a brief overview of the schedule of events goes a long way to increase their comfort level. Don't oversell it; don't undersell it; have as few surprises as possible. Talk about the fun things in store like "you'll meet lots of new children" rather than, "you're going to the ski school," and "you'll have fun in the snow, skiing" rather than, "they will teach you how to ski." If guidelines are not already in place, establish some basic directions to, "follow

don't oversell it, don't undersell it

instructions" and "pay attention." Finally, even though you will be gone all day, promise to return.

The worst thing for a child is a promise that isn't going to happen. Don't say, "I'll be there all day with you," if you won't be there. When the child gets the expectation that Mom and Dad won't leave and finds out they are gone, it creates a greater impact than if the truth were told in the beginning. Secondly, you enter your child into ski school so that they can enjoy a magnificent winter activity and experience the mountain with you. Don't worry if the child isn't picking it up at the rate that you would like them to, if it takes five days to get down the beginner hill, in the big picture it doesn't matter as long as they are enjoying the experience. The flip side of that is tragic, to have a child master the beginner hill in one hour but end up hating the experience with a passion. Just remember that ultimately, they will go up the mountain and ski better than you anyway.

Have a Decent Breakfast

Creating a fertile learning environment starts with showing up on time with the child who has had a decent breakfast. Many times, the children with altitude sickness are in that condition from insufficient sleep, improper hydration and no breakfast. While that diagnosis is for children, it also is an accurate predictor for adults.

53

Children's Progression

At Taos Ski Valley, organized ski school programs begin for children at the age of three, or when they are potty trained. When you consider a group learning situation with strangers, the key is to start only when the child is ready to learn. The best aspects of children learning to ski at Taos are the Ski Week Program and the continuity of the ski experience it offers.

The learning progression for children is essentially the same as it is for adults, but it has been affected by the in-line skating phenomenon. Children should start walking, gliding and then skating around on their skis, so they can always get down the hill. The snow plow or wedge is a very useful technique to compensate for their lack of the necessary muscle development and coordination to ski parallel. Just like using a training wheel on a bike, the snow plow facilitates their skiing experience. However, children can be amazingly versatile, even to the extent of carving beautiful turns in snow-plow position, especially with the new shaped skis.

essentially the same as it is for adults

Early Prime Time

Children are avid learners at any age, but the years between eight and twelve seem to be especially important to motor skill development. Experience has shown that if they learn the fundamentals correctly, then they will develop into much better skiers. The keys during this period are the basics of balance, flexibility, anticipation and pure technique.

Just as the piano scales are important to the pianist, the internalized prime motor skills form the protocol of ski movement patterns and provide a good platform for future progress. The learning environments to which the children are exposed on the mountain can also drive home the fundamentals and should also be as varied as possible with opportunities in the steeps and flats, timed races and free skiing, hard packed snow and soft powder, in good weather as well as bad. Variety actually promotes comprehension just as the social interaction and camaraderie can expand the child's ability to apply the principles further. By far the most important aspect of their learning experience is free skiing. They should ski and ski and ski some more, because nothing beats going down the hill.

> **they should ski and ski and ski some more**

54

Children Are Natural Athletes

Children are natural athletes who learn quickly. "Natural" is so powerful a concept that you use it to teach adults and try to facilitate learning by bringing out the inner child in them. Since children are so natural, they have an intuitive feel for what they are supposed to be doing. For example, when you put skis on them, they realize that they are supposed to go down the hill. And it is only when they get going that they wonder how they are going to stop. When you put an adult on skis, before they ever consider going down the hill they start examining the consequences of the journey like, how am I going to stop? Or, what happens if I fall? These thoughts squish that inner child and retard natural athleticism.

In-line skating and skate boarding are amazing phenomena that have accelerated the learning curve for children. You can find seven-year-old skaters that will pick up skiing far quicker than those children who have not had any in-line skating experience, literally skiing within an hour.

The two key ingredients for children skiing are fun and

learning. Start out with their comfort, which on the mountain is the fundamental issue, then go naturally to the limits of what they can do. For without limits, their innate exuberance might couple with their natural curiosity to produce disaster.

Perhaps the biggest mistake with children is trying to teach them something. The key is to trick them into learning. The distinction between the two concepts is important, because what we try to teach the children is not important, it is what they learn that is crucial.

> **the biggest mistake . . . is trying to teach them something**

55

Children Learn Through Their Bodies

With children it is important not to get bogged down in dogma. It's about movement, so keep them moving at all times. As soon as they can control their speed, turns will almost come naturally because of the edging action that they have learned while in-line skating. Very little time is spent on discussing or learning technique with children. A lot of time is spent on the mountain enjoying the terrain, experimenting with the different snow conditions, and sticking with the common theme of fun and learning.

Children will learn more from the mountain through their bodies, than they will ever learn through their ears. They will learn by watching and imitating, but rarely have the concentration to be coached through the nuances of technique. Children can be tricked into learning through ski drills or other creative activities that will help them absorb, without understanding why or how. It is a "just do it" kind of attitude.

Attitude is important to learning, so treat children like adults and adults like children. In other words, the way to lose children is by a condescending attitude. The way to communicate with children is to approach them from the viewpoint of their understanding, while you treat them like real people. Since children are fantastic little learning machines, they respond to that style of teaching.

keep them moving at all times

56

The Role Of The Parent In Children's Skiing

The image of an out-of-control baseball dad or screaming soccer mom is an example of what can do more harm than good. In skiing, the highest quality support that you could give a child is proper preparation. By addressing the basic needs of food, fluids, sun screen, eye wear, proper clothing and adequate rest, the child has at least an even chance to handle the mountain and is not predisposed to failure. The worst example of this was the family that drove straight from Houston at sea level to Taos Ski Valley at 9300 feet elevation, nonstop and all through the night. En route the entourage was sustained by a solid diet of sugar, junk food and caffeine, yet they wondered why all the kids had altitude sickness upon arrival. Fluids and plenty of them plus adequate rest would have made most people fit to master the hill.

If they don't want to ski, they won't.

By far the best physical preparation for skiing is any physical activity except Nintendo. In-line skating and ice skating are unparalleled as a great preparation for skiing. Bicycling, soccer, football, basketball, swimming, gymnastics or anything that has demands on the legs and the torso will help the body get ready. The more active the child has been, the better the adjustment to skiing.

Psychologically, you should remember that you want the child to be involved just for the fun of it. Pure, unabashed fun. You are not preparing the child for the World Cup, therefore, any pressure to perform can stifle this flower from growing, much less blooming. The big issue at the Taos Ski Valley Children's Center is the social interaction. Children who have been socially interacting with other children and adults usually do better that those that don't have that background.

If you want your children to begin skiing at an early age, expose them to the elements early. Children should be brought up to the mountains early to become acclimated, especially if they normally don't have snow. Let them watch people skiing and see the fun they are having; let them recognize that this is a nice environment.

Perhaps the most important single thing to avoid is the child unwilling to ski — if they don't want to, don't make them. Until they ask, they are not ready. Children can't be brought in kicking and screaming and be expected to come out skiing. You'll find the largest assortment of self-induced maladies from stomach aches to diarrhea, nausea to screaming fits, that children develop to manipulate the situation. If they don't want to ski, they won't.

57

How Long Is Best

Timing is also important for the child's skiing experience: when to ski and how long is best. The biggest crowds at any resort are always between Christmas and New Year's or during spring break. Families have the best experience when there are fewer crowds and more room both on the slopes and in the village. Taos is well known as a resort without large crowds and congestion.

Children need adequate time to be in the environment and on the mountain skiing, in order to learn how to ski. Good things take time. Rarely does a short two-day fling do much for the child's long-term competency build-up. The full-week vacation, on the other hand, allows the child to blossom in the full radiance that only time can nurture, and is far better than taking a couple long weekends.

Good things take time.

A full week provides time to get used to the altitude and time for the repetition of ski technique to build muscle memory and instinctive reaction. Longer periods of time simply lead to more success than shorter periods by adding one success upon another as the formula for enduring progress. The whole family will prosper as well from this approach for it is the parental fears that need to be assuaged by familiarity, and the sore muscles of the siblings that can be relaxed with time. Even the anxiety of separation from the workplace fades by total immersion into the mind-rejuvenating fun of skiing.

Wow,
it does look like fun!

"What do you do that is special," Jerry held Meredith's hand and looked at Jean, "when you are teaching these youngsters to ski? At four years old, Meredith is now a pretty good little soccer player, but she has never been here on the snow." The sun was warming the threesome as they stood on the steps of the St. Bernard Hotel watching skiers finish their runs off the hill.

Jean Mayer, now in his forty-fifth year as Technical Director of the famous Taos Ski Valley Ski School, had seen more than a few anxious young fathers bringing their daughters in for their first lesson. "For a child, what really matters is to build confidence and let them have fun in the experience on the skis," he put his hand on Meredith's chin and looked at her ever-widening eyes, "First, you will have to feel comfortable and warm in your new ski outfit, and know that this is more of a game, and a time to have fun with other little boys and girls just like you, as you play with your skis on, in the snow."

"Wow, it does look like fun," Meredith was amazed as she watched the skiers swish by.

Jean reassured Jerry, "Usually they are a little afraid of the speed and not being able to stop, so we use all kinds of techniques to control their gliding. Sometimes we hold them, sometimes we put a little strap around their waist so that we can let them glide in front of us. We talk to them all the time as they are gently gliding down the hill. They like to know what is going on."

As proprietor of the St. Bernard, Jean had many guests skiing on the hill, and watched a few hot shots come off the bumps in front of the hotel. "Progressively we get the children used to the sensation of gliding with speed, and then we start to control that element of speed with some sort of run out."

"Run out," Jerry asked, "you mean the long flat at the bottom of the hill?"

"Exactly. And since we will have her on fairly short skis, she will be able to move around quite easily." Jean pointed at his skis, "The new technology of these skis is absolutely wonderful. More maneuverable, lighter, easier to turn. A few years ago, I would have been on 190-centimeter skis whereas now I am on a 158. The same goes for the children; it is now a lot easier for them to ski."

"How do you get them to pay attention?" Jerry looked at his daughter as she watched the skiers.

"We keep it stress-free and we keep the kids into it at all times. We never use technical terms but rather talk about their skis and the snow . . . the things that they are familiar with. And we never use baby talk." Jean continued, "The child's first day on the snow is very important, and our instructors are excellent in handling that sensitively. They try everything to make the children feel at ease. We even have a special little people-mover to get the children up the hill without any strain of an old fashioned rope tow or pulley. Children love the idea of walking and moving and being able to get around on their skis."

"So what is the real bottom line?" — the unrelenting business executive kept popping out of Jerry.

"The whole concept that you try to emphasize more than anything else," Jean concluded to Mister Anxious, "is the fun. The more they love it, they more they will ski. Just remember, in a few short years, they will be skiing better than you anyway."

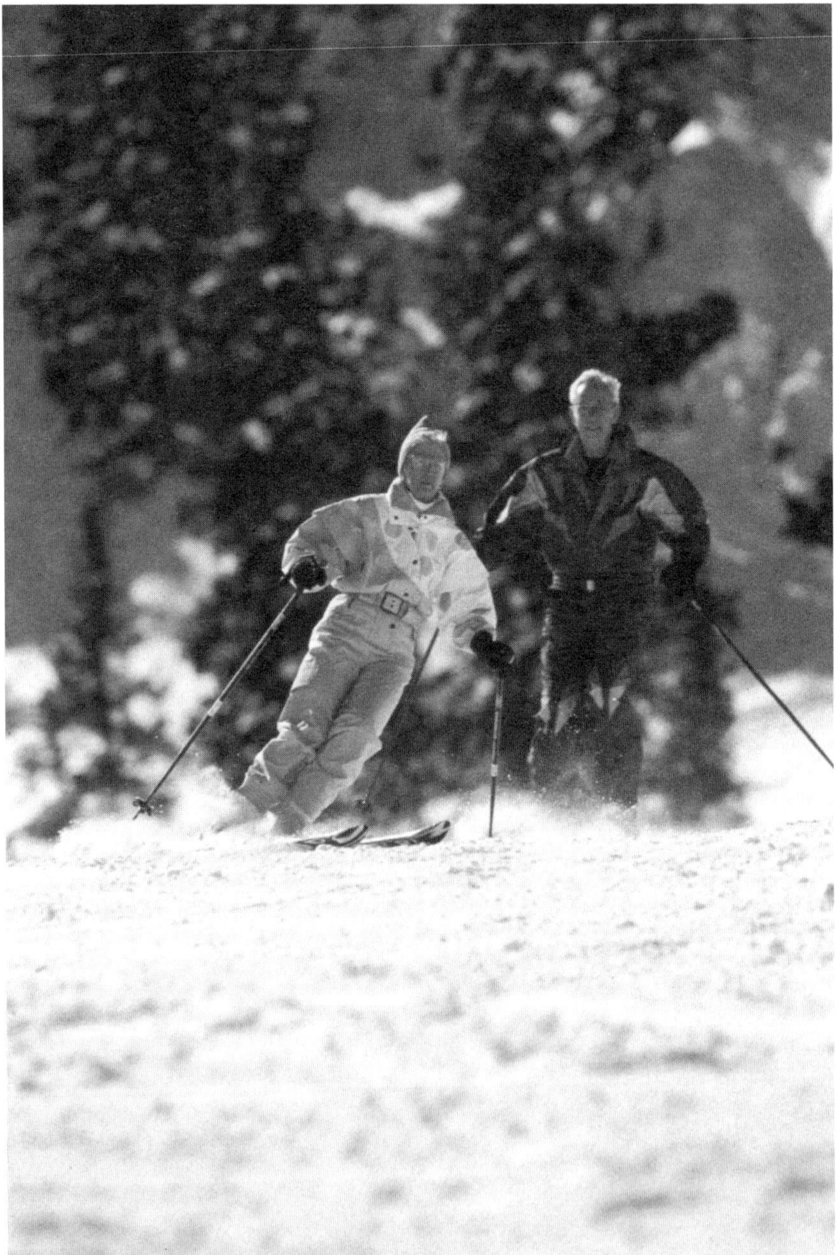

Ninth Run:

Late Bloomers

Motivated by the aura, the majesty, and the thrill.

. . . stretching is more useful than strength.

. . . with the new equipment, skiing is not an ordeal.

. . . the total mountain experience is irresistible.

. . . balance and flexion start with the new equipment.

. . . externally and internally, it's your state of mind.

58

Be Flexible

If you are in your forties, fifties and sixties and want to start skiing, you may be motivated by the aura of the sport, the majesty of the mountains and the thrill of the snow. All are sound reasons. Your concerns relate to safety issues or how to keep from hurting yourself. Being realistic, there are no guarantees that injuries won't occur.

However, be flexible as you approach the hard-core learning issues. Your learning patterns are similar to children's, if you just give yourself a chance. Playing games is a more effective learning scenario with demonstration and discovery, than an in-depth discussion of theory. Certainly you can understand a little more about how the binding works, and why the ski turns, but doing still works best.

So as a latecomer to this snowy stage of experience, don't arrive with preconceived ideas of how the teaching and learning should take place. You may have education ideas straight out of the fifties such as, "Here are the rules. . . ," "Do as I say. . . ," and "Follow these steps." The trouble is, instruction technique has progressed a lot since then, so have patience with a teaching style that may be different from the style you knew.

The best preparation for skiing for your late blooming body is stretching — simple flexibility stretching. Stretching is more useful to you than strength because safety is more important than endurance. Muscles will move and joints will provide the control to do what you have to do to stay safe and enjoy the experience. Five or six days before your first trip to the hill, start some basic rotary exercises to loosen the twisting muscles and not necessarily lengthen them. Learning to ski utilizes some twisting muscles that you probably haven't used before.

Stretching is more useful to you than strength.

59

Cognitive And Comfortable

The self-preservation instinct strengthens every year that you are alive; as a late beginner therefore, you tend to be more cognitive about your skiing. If you have maintained an active lifestyle and have good physical health, learning how to ski won't be an ordeal. Unless, of course, you have laid off physical activity since you were old enough to know better, you now face a twofold challenge of the physical demands exacerbated by the mental anxiety of safety. Fortunately, both are easily overcome.

The new equipment technology has made it easier for you to learn to ski late in life. Boots are more comfortable, skis are shorter, lighter and more responsive, and even the facilities are more user-friendly. Take for instance the TSV Zipper, a specially constructed people-mover, designed to lessen your stress as a new skier, since you will have those encumbrances (skis) strapped to your feet for the first time. Simply stand on

new equipment technology has made it easier for you

the Zipper to take you up the hill without the strain of climbing or the discomfort of a rope tow. This is a huge step, literally, in helping you develop the appropriate skier's equanimity and composure.

60

Escape Versus Anxiety

The Good

As a late starter, the total mountain experience creates an irresistible incentive to ski more. The subtle pleasures of good living are evoked by the whole aura of the mountain scenery, the fresh air, the European atmosphere, the fine meals and the camaraderie. Although the wind in the face and the adrenalin rush of gravity-defying experiences will help you recreate your youth, they tend to be of secondary importance when compared to the spirit and the camaraderie on the mountain.

Skiing is also one of the more convenient ways to appreciate an authentic winter environment without being a polar explorer; especially important if you have lived all your life in the concrete canyons of a major metropolis. Escape is good. When you glide down the slopes of Taos Ski Valley and see no other signs of civilization, you know there is hope for the planet.

Escape is good.

The Bad

Anxiety is bad. The most destructive attitude when learning to ski is unproductive, irrational fear — it can literally cause you to lose the joy of the moment. The good side of fear evolves into common sense; we wish that many teenagers had a greater helping of it. Uncontrolled fear actually can ravage your possibilities of good skiing as a mature starter, so don't let it keep you from what you really could enjoy.

Anxiety is bad.

The Helpful

To leverage the physical basics, you can feed your cognitive side by a healthy diet of visualization and other food for the brain. Watching ski videos and reading inspirational ski material will actually help to prepare you for the mental part of the game. And, it's ok to have a little anxiety rush. Share those feeling with others. You'll be surprised at the number of other people that are having those same feelings.

feed your cognitive side

61

A Balanced And Agile Style

Balance has always made the most sense for every skier, especially the senior variety. This dispels the notion of skiing with your feet together, which was most rampant in the sixties and seventies. Actually then, like now, it was the equipment that actually dictated the style. Picture yourself on eight-foot-long hickory skis with ankle-high leather boots — if you didn't ski with your feet together, you were asking for disaster. In a film of the '64 Olympics, racers were skiing with their boots together and picking up their feet to turn because of the ski's design. Since the skis couldn't edge very well, it took a big strapping athlete to make them look even remotely controllable.

The sixties' style of skiing with the feet together was dictated by the design of the equipment and, when used today, it is more for "form" than function. Just try walking with your feet bound together. Uncomfortable isn't it? Now have someone push you from the side. It is easy to lose balance and hard to stand straight, isn't it? Consider that same scenario on skis, moving smartly down the mountain, navigating snow conditions, people, terrain and weather. Wouldn't it help to have balance and agility? The style that makes the most sense for mature skiers is one that can provide the most range of motion through proper flexing of the ankles, knees and hips. Equipment is now more suited to allow that range of motion. Designers realized that in order to make the ski torsionally stiff, longitudinal stiffness also had to increase so that when the ski is put on its edge, it will stay on its edge. Modern technology uses titanium and carbon fibers everywhere to allow the ski to be flexible yet torsionally stiff. This means the skis will bow when you put pressure on them, yet allow the you to ski on both feet, providing an easier, more stable turn.

> **one that can provide the most range of motion**

Ski boots have also improved. In the old days, the leather boots had to be stiff so that when you pressed into the boot, it bent the ski. Now that skis are more flexible, boots are stiffer laterally and softer on the forward flex, thus more comfortable and very responsive to your ankles.

One of the most valuable recommendations an instructor can make is an appraisal of your personal equipment. By matching equipment to your actual skiing competency, your alignment will be improved and so will your skiing.

62

Enjoy The Experience

Skiing is all about fun, relaxation and enjoyment of external and internal elements. Externally the experience is the mountains — the weather, beauty and freshness — making skiing a memorable sensation; enjoy it. Gliding down the slope is, of course, the main attraction, so do it always in control, at your own comfort level, without unreasonable expectations. Use the terrain to help in all your maneuvers. The mountain is your friend — it provides the slopes that allow you to glide effortlessly; and the same slopes will help you stop and keep in control.

Internally, your enjoyment of skiing depends on your state of mind. Late bloomers should look for less challenge and more fun. Don't expect to be skiing at an Olympic level like a twenty-one-year-old who has been skiing since the age of three. It is rare that nature works like that. You should, however, expect to have great fun, stopping when you're tired and expanding your limits within reason.

do it always in control, at your own comfort level

The Mecca Myth

The most pervasive myth about Taos is that it is a challenging ski mecca which only welcomes a certain type of skier. It certainly is a ski mecca, but it is accessible to all types of skiers. All ages of guests enjoy their experience more because it is a "ski only" crowd.

I can't believe
I skied the steeps

Helen skied up to Jeff and looked straight at him with a twinkle in her eyes, "You'll never know how much you helped me," she confided. "This was my first time in any ski school, and I've never before skied five days in a row. I thought I was kind of an intermediate, but skiing the icy hills of northern Ohio is hardly worth comparing. And even though I'm not in the shape that I should be, I can't believe I've skied something so incredibly steep."

"The first time always looks steep here," Jeff Mugleston knew the feeling well, although it had been thirty years since he first came to Taos. Now as one of the ski school managers, he still likes to teach a class personally, in the tradition that Jean Mayer as Technical Director set for the instructors years ago. "In comparison to the hills of Ohio, this may look steep, but as you have seen, it is really a piece of cake. You've progressed so much during this Ski Week, no one can believe the difference!"

"It was only last Monday that I was freaking out when we took our first warmup run down Porcupine. I thought I was going to die," she beamed.

This is what Jeff loves to hear from his students, "You learned that the secret to skiing is your control of speed, and speed is controlled by the way you turn. Point the skis down the hill and you will pick up speed; aim them back up the hill and you will stop.

But most importantly, you accomplished what you came to do, you had a tremendous time, made some great new friends, and you skied like you have never skied before."

"I wasn't exactly aiming for the Olympics, but I was amazed in where we went and how comfortable I felt in what I did. What an experience; they won't believe it back home!"

182

Tenth Run:

The New Equipment allows you to do more than ever before.

To improve your skiing and re-energize your spirits.

. . . for the mature, new equipment adds ten + years.

. . . the stress is less and the control is more.

. . . the intermediate skis better, the master skis longer.

. . . you can now arc a turn almost too effortlessly.

. . . arrive in shape and be self-aware.

63

Shorter Is Better

The advances in the design of new equipment have revolutionized skiing. Skis are shorter and much more shaped to allow you to do more than they ever were able to before. Certainly there have been excesses perpetrated on us by some of the manufacturers, but shaped skis allow you to perform better and quicker, as well as to enjoy the process and the mountain more. This equipment allows the instructors to spend more time on the important feelings and sensations of the guests' instruction rather than solely on the technique.

You will find out how it feels to defy gravity, to lean and touch the snow in the turn. Practically, the new equipment also adds ten to fifteen years of additional skiing for mature skiers, who are now able to do things that they could only wish for before this new technology.

find out how it feels to defy gravity

64

It May Be Easier, And It Sure Is Better

The new equipment has profoundly affected the expectations of all who ski on them; all age and ability levels seem to be getting better performance out of their skis. Starting at the most basic level, enjoyment has increased because the stress is less — you have increased control of your skis and decreased physical exertion on them. There is a whole new atmosphere of almost giddy pleasure associated with skis that are designed to turn, on easy bindings, and in comfortable boots.

New equipment has allowed virtually everyone to ski at a higher level than they previously could have achieved. The new technology has even converted the old-timers who grew up with primitive equipment into users who stresslessly agree, "it may be easier but it certainly is better."

> a whole new atmosphere of almost giddy pleasure

Instructors can now work with their students in a much more natural way. For years and years they told their students what seemed to be a counter-intuitive direction for proper turning, i.e., lean against the turn instead of with the turn. The counter-intuitive aspect of that advice becomes clearer when you consider a skater's movement into a turn is just that — leaning into the turn. Previous skiing instruction had students leaning from the waist up to the outside — to angulate — which is a counter-intuitive movement.

Another movement required by the technology of the old equipment had skiers sometimes rotating their bodies against the direction they were turning. These same instructors told students to keep the inside ski off the snow and keep all weight on the outside ski as they described a proper turn. A turn they even demonstrated while balanced on the outside ski holding the inside ski more than a foot off the ground.

Today, instructors encourage you to maintain support on the inside ski in contact with the snow. The technology improvements have significantly changed ski technique.

65

More Natural, And Sometimes Less Physical

Modern equipment is now light years beyond equipment of just a few years ago. The previous equipment was physical: it required speed and power to turn, and the only people carving were the experts. Current ski equipment design and materials allow even beginner-level skiers to use the ski design to turn effortlessly.

The length of skis has been dramatically affected by the technology revolution. In 1990, an advanced skier was skiing a 200-centimeter ski; in 2002, that same skier might be skiing anything from a 158- to a 188-cm ski, dependent on the normal variables of height, weight, type of ski, type of terrain or personal preference. Stable performance with more control is the astronomical benefit from the shorter, lighter and more maneuverable configurations. That means more fun on the skinny chutes, or tree lines that seemed impossible, or the groomed runs that needed speed.

The net effect of the more compact equipment is a bonanza for the beginner: less length to encumber movement on the slopes; more maneuverability and control for easier learning; and lighter weight to decrease fatigue and stress. A beginner skier who started on a 160-cm ski in 1990 would start on a 120- or a 130-cm ski today. More importantly, the new equipment has allowed the movements of skiing to be more natural. Today, the beginner learns faster, the intermediate skis better, the masters ski longer, and the experts ski absolutely everything. Taos recognized and adopted this natural technique early on and led the industry in actually teaching it before the equipment arrived. Now, that's a trick.

stable performance with more control

Proper Fitting

Since proper functioning equipment is so important in skiing, the best time a beginner could invest in learning is the time spent in the ski shop on the hill. They will check body alignment with the fit of the boot and make sure your ability level is matched for the type of ski and pole that you use. No matter what your age when you ski for the first time, a proper fitting in your ski boot will increase your odds of having a great experience.

Equipment For Children

"Let's buy boots one or two sizes larger than they need

now, so it will last through next season . . ." How many times have you heard that or said it yourself? It may work for sweaters but it doesn't work for ski boots. Children grow so quickly that if you try to anticipate the future growth spurts, it will result in misfitting both then and now. Fitting children into boots is always a challenge — boots must be soft enough with adequate back support, yet allow a good range for ankle flexion. Since children have a great sense of balance but do not have a great deal of muscle mass, their boots cannot be too stiff, for then they won't allow adequate forward flex. When the shin presses against the front tongue of the boot, the child's center of balance will be forced to the rear which will ultimately make it difficult to turn. With the new shorter skis, children must start turns with their balance forward so that they can finish the turn being centered. In order to allow this natural movement to shift their balance forward, children need boots that will help center them. Being centered is the bottom line for all turns by anyone, and proper boot fitting is one the major contributors to being centered.

Ski rental equipment is so good and affordable now that most children will use better equipment, while the parents spend less money, by using the rental shop.

children need boots that will help center them

66

Park and Ride — A Misnomer

Since the new skis are much shorter, well tapered and with more side-cut, when they are put on their edge, they are easier to carve with less skidding and pivoting. With a lighter swing weight, it is easier to steer the ski quickly into the new turn for added dimension of skiing versatility.

Skiing on the new equipment has become deceptively easy to the point of causing a syndrome unheard of just a few short years ago called, "Park and Ride." Skiers and even some instructors use the new technology to park their bodies on the ski edge as they ride down the hill, but are forgetting how to carve a turn properly. New skis allow you to arc a turn effortlessly, but be careful not to miss the subtlety of true carving — by engaging those skis on edge to come out of the turn with more energy, momentum and constant acceleration. The shape of the new skis allows you to let your skis move further out and your center of mass further in. With the right timing and movement, this can lead to great carving turns.

> **be careful not to miss the subtlety of true carving**

Extend Your Arc

New technology allows this additional flexibility to put the ski on edge, but the real secret of carving unfolds in the completion of the turn, a little further extension of the arc to produce more energy out of the turn. The sooner you can arc at the top of the turn, the more speed you'll pick up in the turn, the more you will balance yourself against the effects of the turn, and the less you'll have to fight to keep yourself in balance.

Edge Early

The key to carving a turn is to put your ski on edge as early as possible. If you need to tighten the radius of the turn, just press the tip of the ski more and the turn will be shorter. After you are on edge, you are in control because you are balanced against the platform you established when you set up your edge at the top of the arc. Do all of this before you cross the fall line so that when you pass it, you can seamlessly transition to the next turn, carrying your momentum with you. From one fall line to the next fall line, set your edge early to complete your turn fast and gain power down the slope.

67

Athleticism Disguised

A common problem in preparing for skiing is not wanting to do as much as you know is necessary to arrive in shape and survive on the slope. Running, interval training, and weights provide the basics, but by tricking the mind and disguising training as fun, the rigors of the routine can be made more palatable.

Basic athletic training will develop the ski-specific muscles you require to enjoy skiing more. Running allows you to develop the slow twitch muscles and lungs necessary for endurance. Interval training strengthens your heart, weights develop power, stretching prevents injury plus speeds recovery from the strenuous effort, and plyometry quickens muscular reaction.

develop the ski-specific muscles

Conditioning your body is easier when a playful approach converts exercises into entertainment, such as practicing balance by walking on a log or jumping from rock to rock. Try standing on one foot and balancing without touching the ground as you slip on your socks or stockings in the morning. Your foot, ankle and calf muscles will each get a workout as they try to maintain your equilibrium. And for the coup de grace, try lacing your shoe balancing on one foot. Each day you will strengthen more muscles and reactions.

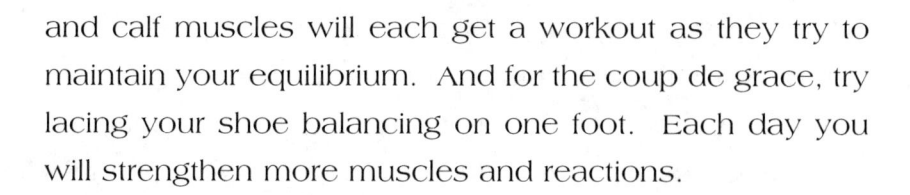

Physically, Don't Cheat Yourself

Physically, the best preparation for skiing is all-around body conditioning. In order to ski you must have flexibility and strength, endurance and quick reactions, balance and body awareness. A certain amount of self-discipline will greatly enhance your skiing pleasure, and allow you to achieve a deeper awareness of who you really are.

If you consider the money invested on a ski holiday, why not go a step further and learn how to get the most out of all your equipment and enjoy the entire experience as much as you can. Better preparation is the secret.

> **self-discipline will greatly enhance your skiing pleasure**

The Big WHY And The Big WHAT

The key to better mental preparation is self-awareness. Find out why you are doing what you are doing. The big

WHY and the big WHAT. What turns you on? Why do you do this? Do you enjoy it or are you scared? And if so why? How can you communicate the reasons better so you can get over it? You can improve your self-awareness with an open mind, less ego to look dispassionately at your problems, and an open ear to hear possible solutions. By the same token, you should not be too hard on yourself nor too demanding. Always make room for something totally new and different in your life.

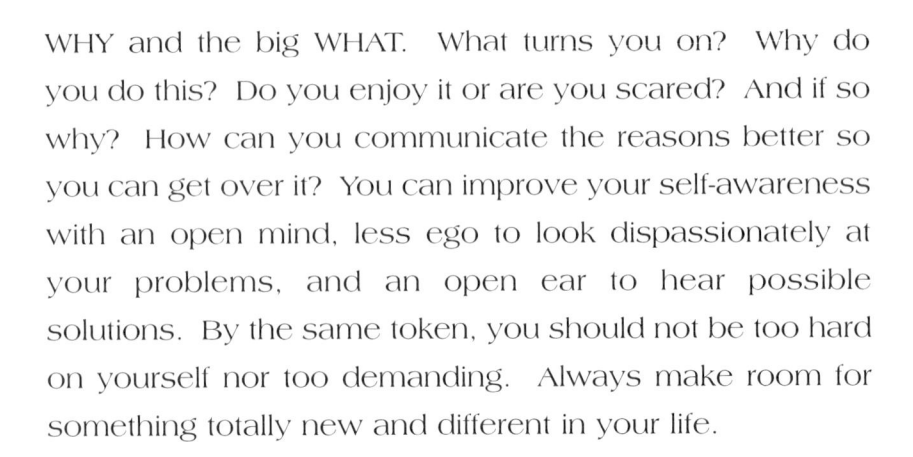

you should not be too hard on yourself

Nostalgia seems to be on a fast track back; many people have found that there is too much technology engulfing us and affecting how we enjoy life. Sometimes technology erases the basic joy of simple pleasures except in skiing. Skiing equipment has changed for the better, and the change allows us to enjoy the basic pleasure even more.

Stir Your Juices

Since emotions play a big part in learning, you should also use them in the preparation for skiing. It is O.K. to anticipate the adventure and the massive departure from the norm that can stir your soul. Getting psyched up is also acceptable — when you stir your emotional soul juices, you will unearth new potential within yourself. Your pre-skiing anticipation will also accentuate the deep emotional reward and satisfaction from doing something that is physically demanding. This may not appeal to everyone, but to those whose deck it shuffles, it provides a winner every time.

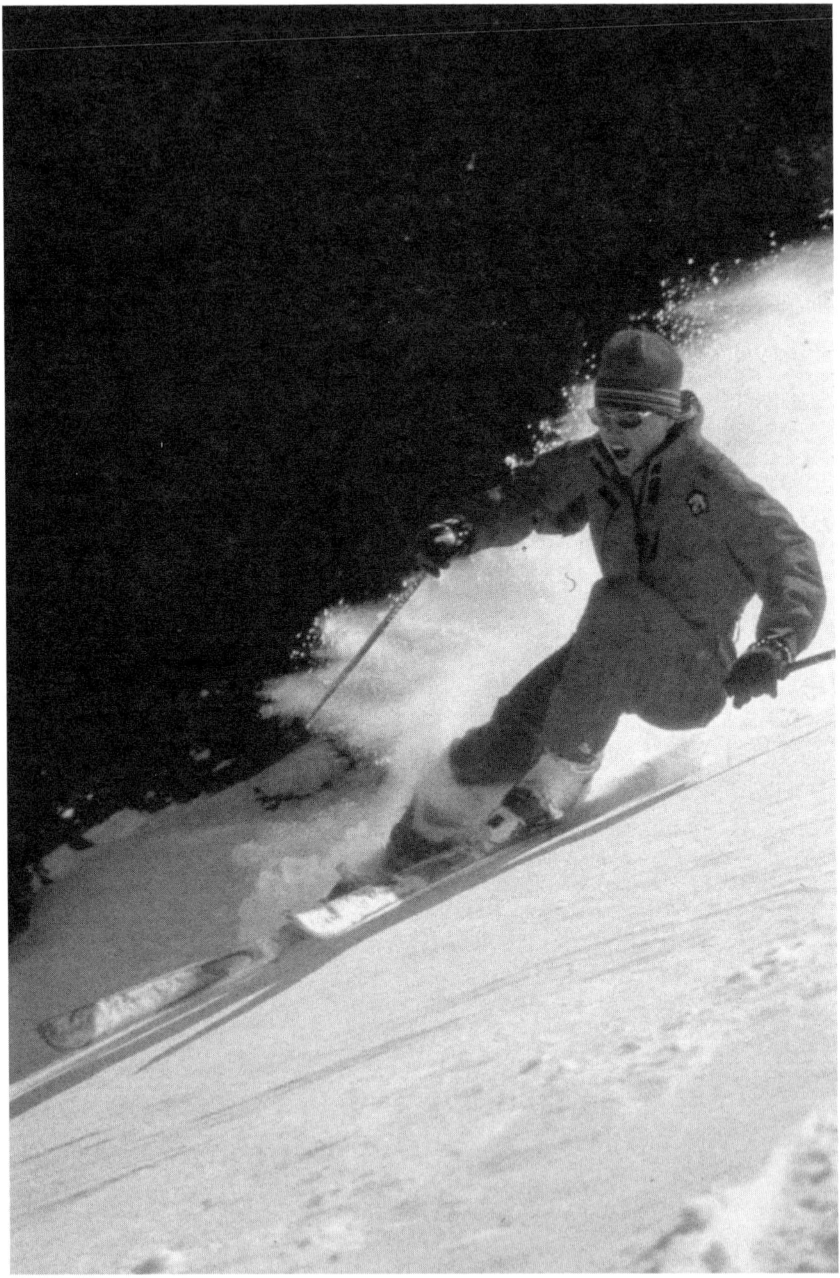

Eleventh Run:

High-Performance Skiing

The mental aspects are most important.

. . . the difference between achievers and the also-ran.

. . . think about what to accomplish; focus on the ideas.

. . . watch what you say; give yourself a cue.

. . . react to fear with aggressiveness, sharpness and intensity.

. . . an aid to self-confidence and the power of the process.

. . . be careful of self-imposed limits that show up as attitudes.

. . . totally in the moment to just have fun.

68

Visual Imagery – See Yourself

When you consider the demands of high-performance skiing at the World Cup or Olympic level, the mental aspects are perhaps the most important difference between the achievers and the also-ran. Debbie Armstrong, Gold Medalist in the Sarajevo Olympics, has achieved the highest recognition in the sport and is a world-class athlete. Overall mental preparation and the use of visual imagery were some of the factors of her ability to achieve peak performance, consistently. Many elite athletes at the top of their game use visualization as one of the tools to leverage their performance level.

Even for the non-world-class skier, visualization can be used at the top of the run to anticipate and preview what is ahead if the run is familiar, or to review technique positions and attitude adjustments. You can use visual imagery as if you were watching a movie of yourself coming down Al's Run, or you can view it through your own eyes, as if you were doing it yourself in realtime. The latter, or first person approach, is the more preferred way because you can experience the mental stimulation and physical sensations, complete with a minimal amount of muscle firing, even to the extent of a little adrenalin kicking in. You end up actually rehearsing the run or technique and thus practicing the focus necessary to execute flawlessly, plus anticipating physical demands to gear up your muscles for the action.

one of the tools to leverage their performance level

The best example of the benefits of the power of visual imagery was when Debbie hurt herself on the U.S. Ski Team and couldn't practice for two months. She realized that there was homework for her next race — visual imagery — to be done while she was laid up, which could be a major part of her recovery. Daily she would run gates in her mind to feel the carved turns, see the gates, experience as many of the physical sensations and techniques as she could and keep her mental abilities sharp. So when the time came for her first race, against her fellow U.S. Ski Team members who had been skiing all winter long, she won. Without any doubt, Debbie attributes that success to her mental preparation.

69

Plan Your Run

Like any mental technique, visual imagery applied to skiing takes time to develop, practice and internalize. It's too late if you try to use it in the middle of your time of need, when you have never tried it before. Consider a practical, smaller scale way to begin your mental preparation routine to expand your envelope of ski performance. Before you start the run, pause for a second to develop a plan by thinking about one or two things you would like to accomplish initially. Focus on the ideas and imagine what you would do to put yourself one step ahead of the game; and feel your muscles tingle with anticipation as they fire up waiting to go. You now have a double-edged tool to help you succeed, with one side of sharpened focus and the other side of pointed physical alertness. Do this consistently, run after run, until you automatically formulate a plan for what you will do. Plan your run, and run your plan.

When the run is over, think about what you did well and what you did poorly. Try to figure out why, and more importantly, how to repeat the good things and correct the things that were bad. Your objective is to be conscious about your actions, so you can plan better and be as good as you can be.

70

Fear Not

The concept of visual imagery is not only for the physical and the mental application of technique but also for the psychological aspect of the experience. You can imagine the fears that you will be experiencing — the pressure of people watching (such as under the lift on Reforma) or skiing with you, noises such as the sliding on ice, or the sting of blowing snow — their affect on the outcome and their distraction or motivation. By identifying these potentially disruptive forces as a part of your preparation, they will be less destructive to your focus when you are actually skiing and performing in the moment.

by identifying disruptive forces . . .they will be less destructive

And Seldom Was Heard A Discouraging Word

One of the last things that Debbie told herself before leaving the starting gate in Sarajevo was, "Have fun." She wasn't out of her mind but rather really into her mind, because she was imbedding a subliminal command to relax and enjoy doing what her plan and practice led her there to do. This was a gentle reminder right before she shot down the hill that, after all, this was just a sport and she was there having the time of her life.

Positive affirmations are one of the most important types of self-talk that you can use to improve your performance. Start by identifying any form of negative self-talk and replacing it with something positive. Negative self-talk is pernicious because of its subtlety and pervasiveness. Even relatively innocent statements such as, "... that wasn't very good," or "... don't do that, you dummy," or ". . . stupid, stupid, stupid" are lethal when repeated over and over again. Any good coach would never say that to you or any other athlete to inspire greater performance; it would be deflating, rude and disrespectful. It only makes sense to treat yourself the same way, always being nice, respectful and motivational.

On the other hand, an effective coach would probably say something positive to draw the best out of an athlete: ". . . Now why don't you try this," or ". . . I like what you are doing there, but think about doing this." Do the same thing with yourself, using positive self-talk as an important part of your plan for the run, whether it is psyching yourself up or not psyching yourself down. Positive self-talk can do wonders to build the right attitude, such as, "I can do this," or ". . . I've done this before; I can do this again," or ". . . focus, focus, I can do it."

always being nice, respectful and motivational

Any type of negative talk often precipitates the disaster that it refers to, ". . . last time I did this I fell," or ". . . they're watching; I don't like the pressure" or " . . . I don't know if I can do this." The negatives often instigate the problem or at least undermine the attitude that lets the original plan succeed.

Don't be Cueless

The definition of a cue in theatrical circles is the last word that indicates the time for the next person to act or speak. In the mental preparation for skiing, it works the same way. During practice, consistently repeat a cue word either to precede a specific action or to change your thought about a negative image, so that your body will be stimulated to a movement or an action. Some people call this Pavlov's theory, and of course they are right. In skiing or any sport, a cue word can define a problem or action response.

An example of the effective use of cue words came early in Debbie's racing career. She had a tendency to use the back half of her ski and to sit far back in her boots. The corrective action was to move her hips forward so that she could better engage the tips of her skis and make use of her full ski. Her cue words while skiing the mountain were, "Hips up," so that she could immediately identify what she had to do to improve her position — move her hips up to better engage her skis.

A cue word is a simple quick code that can inspire a position or body movement or even an attitudinal change. If thoughts about falling flood your mind every time you come to a certain type of geographic feature or every time you attempt a certain technique, change the picture on your mental screen. Your body will move and your mind will change from a code word that is practiced to evoke a more positive and more reassuring visual.

a simple quick code that can inspire

71

A Fearsome Focus

This is not an area for people with poor reality-acceptance skills. Fear is good, healthy and a part of our psychological makeup for good reason. It is important to have a sense of your abilities' level and your bodily response to fear. If, for example, your heart quickens its pace and your breathing becomes faster in the time of fear, you know then to focus on breathing, taking those deep and long breaths that are soothing. Or if negative self-talk is your first response to fear, ". . . Oh my gosh, I am going to crash . . . ," you'll want to reorient your response pattern to construct a performance-sustaining if not performance-enhancing thought. In time of fear, think about what is important to become successful, and not what will detract from your ability to succeed.

One of the common physical responses to fear in skiing is to tighten up, become static, reduce flexion, get stiff and lean back. This defensive attitude may cause you to fall back on the wrong instincts and exacerbate their negative effects on your technique.

Debbie has trained herself to have a completely

opposite reaction to fear while she is skiing through extra aggressiveness, sharpness and intensity of overall focus. One of her favorite examples was during a World Cup downhill race, while going seventy miles per hour approaching a waterfall of a bump, she knew that if she took it wrong, she would launch herself and lose valuable time floating airborne. A defensive position over the bump would lose the race for her, assuming that she would even survive the fall. She gave herself the opportunity to be successful by being aggressive, balanced, focused and ready to go for it.

Being defensive rarely is an advantage in skiing.

Being defensive rarely is an advantage in skiing. As long as your reality-acceptance skills are installed and operative, your knowledge of your strengths and weaknesses will help you avoid situations that are above your competency level. And with the help of an instructor, you can push yourself and be aggressive to go to places and do things that you have never done before.

72

A Goal Habit

Debbie was aware of the power of goal-setting even as a junior racer. When she was eighteen, she told her parents that she had never set a goal that she did not reach. She got into the habit of setting realistic goals and reaching them to develop self-confidence. On the U.S. Ski Team, she made so many of the goals that she set — that it gave her even more confidence in the power of the process. It was awesome for her to realize that if she was willing to set something as a goal for herself, she could attain it.

Goal-setting for Debbie also helped her realize what was doable and what was not. The most frequent problem is setting

> **realize what was doable and what was not**

goals that are too lofty, without the incremental goals that make them possible. If you do not include the incremental goals as a part of your everyday experience, they will never become a habit.

As a nineteen-year-old, Debbie did not have the Olympic Gold Medal as a goal; it was too lofty, unattainable and unthinkably optimistic. However, she did her homework every day — all the little things that champions do to be as good as they can be — and consequently beat everyone that she competed against. She made each of her goals realistic and reachable, and habitually worked to attain them — and did it all at the age of twenty, when she won the gold.

73

You Didn't Know You Weren't Supposed To Win

As a result of society, family, friends, coaches, teammates or even themselves, athletes tend to suffer from self-inflicted performance limits. Sometimes these performance limits come disguised as the "rules" or the customary "way things are." In football, rarely is the third-string quarterback the MVP of the Super Bowl. In basketball, Michael Jordan doesn't lose a game of one-on-one to a kid in the local gym. Anytime these rules change, the difference is noted and the occasion is celebrated.

Self-imposed limits also show up as attitudes, like "I've never been able to do this in the past; why should I be able to do it now?" Or, "I'm not as good an athlete as he is, so I can't do this." The self-limiting attitudes develop subtly or suddenly as a result of a traumatic event, but nonetheless restrict your achievement level.

Debbie's most striking example of no self-limitations was at the age of eighteen, in her first World Cup race in Saalbach, Austria. Fresh from the United States, she was not familiar with the World Cup circuit at all. This city kid from Seattle did not know any of the racers, what they looked like or even their names, much less any of the "rules." Debbie's starting position was 65th in a field of 72. Despite all odds and so blissful in her ignorance, she proceeded to win her first training run, which was unheard of: a newcomer didn't do that.

At the end of the day, she called her parents to announce the news, to which her father questioned, "How do you feel about that?"

Debbie responded, "I feel fine, but everyone else around me is freaking out!"

"Well Deb," he said, "you didn't know that you weren't supposed to win."

This was so important a statement to Debbie Armstrong that she later mused that she could put it on her gravestone. It had major impact because she finally realized that anything was possible. She won that run because she didn't know that she wasn't supposed to!

From that point on she was actually afraid to set goals for herself that might place limits on what she could achieve. A goal is an expectation, but could you exceed it? If you committed to one level of achievement, maybe you are not giving yourself proper credit to accomplish a higher level of performance? It may be a cliché to say, "Where there is a will, there is a way," but it works. Why place limits?

To be open-minded is more than a platitude. If you are not open-minded, you will impose limits on yourself directly or indirectly by not considering expansion opportunities. Debbie has endless examples of her students breaking through self-imposed limitations because the students allowed her to expose them to new areas on the mountain that they would never have considered in the past. The operative concept is that the mountain is the teacher and the instructor is the coach and the guide.

Gordon Briner summed this up simply, "If you don't have confidence, you won't be comfortable in your skiing and you won't achieve breakthrough performance. You must free yourself of self-imposed limits and be strong in your mind that you can accomplish your goal."

if you are not open-minded, you will impose limits

74

The Gold of Sarajevo

Debbie definitely had a plan for that day in Sarajevo — to come home with the Gold. But the plan was largely a mental rather than a technical approach, with three key components: The first leg of her plan was to get to the bottom of the hill and not wish for a second chance. As the hinge pin of her strategy for the race, she knew that most people would only get one shot at an opportunity like the Olympics, so she needed to make the most of it. She had to be totally in the moment and not thinking of what she could or could not do — not about fear, apprehension, or the eventual outcome. Her only focus was skiing as well as she could.

> **a mental rather than a technical approach**

Secondly, Debbie knew that this race was going to be different from anything that she had yet experienced. The next part of her race plan then was to recognize that difference and revel in it, to experience every aspect of this unique moment and love it. By frolicking in the experience, she diffused the stressful, introspective, negative thoughts of, "This is the Olympics, there is a lot of pressure here . . . there's a lot of people watching . . . how am I going to handle this . . . " and allowed her to stay in the moment, totally psyched to achieve peak performance.

"Just have fun" was the last aspect of the strategy, because it was the reason she was there in the first place. This element unfortunately is forgotten many times by many people, whether it is the World Cup Race or Al's Run. You ski for the fun of it, however you define "fun."

Down the hill
with Debbie

"What incredible enthusiasm for skiing! It's a love and passion for skiing that bubbles over and affects all who are around her," said Gordon Briner, General Manager of Taos Ski Valley, with a gentle smile. "Debbie has an exuberance and an excitement that shows immediately in her form and action, if you can keep up with her to notice."

"She is quite adventurous and aggressive in challenging herself with the mountain. Her forte has been racing at incredible speeds, over torturous terrain and under tremendous pressure," Gordon continued. "She shines on the steeps and bumps and the real signature stuff that Taos legends are made of." Yet Debbie's calm, reassuring way in dealing with all types of skiers, at any level of competency, offers to each of them a glimpse of what is the top of the class!

This truly is what Taos is all about. It is the love for the total experience of the mountain, magical in its mystery, enthralling in its majesty, bewitching in its charm. While the total skiing adventure takes the challenge, it leverages it with a special camaraderie that results in the soul-penetrating, mind-altering reward of The Art Of Skiing – Taos.

INDEX

A
Act of love — 49

Advanced skiing at Taos — 17

Adventure skiing — 59, 107, 123, 124, 126, 130, 135, 138, 140, 144

Alignment — 90, 92, 98, 177, 188

Anxiety — 88, 96, 147, 153, 164, 172, 174, 175

Arc — 105, 112, 113, 183, 190, 191

Armstrong, Debbie — 8, 18, 23, 72, 198, 211

Art — 8-12, 14, 16, 17, 20, 36-38, 49, 82, 215

Artist — 25, 43, 46

Attitude — 32, 38, 54, 68, 72, 80, 96, 100, 113, 115, 123, 126, 132, 136, 159, 175, 197, 198, 204, 206

Avalanche — 125, 126, 136, 137

B
Balance — 82, 90, 93, 94, 113, 115, 142, 150, 156, 169, 176, 189, 193

Bend your knees — 107

Big purist mountain — 36

Blake, Ernie — 13, 27, 28, 41, 45, 50, 52, 67, 117-120

Body awareness — 37, 87, 96, 193

Briner, Gordon — 8, 14, 212, 215

Bumps — 89, 103-109, 111, 113, 135, 140, 166, 215

C
Centering — 87, 95, 127, 150

Children — 148-163, 165-167, 188, 189

Children's progression — 155

Commitment — 54, 77, 96, 137

Crud — 75, 127, 133, 140, 141

D
DeCoursey, Doug — 8, 17, 104

E
Edge first — 105, 106

Ego — 31, 38, 88

Endurance — 171, 192, 193

Equilibrium — 193

Equipment for children — 188

F
Fear — 72, 107, 175, 202, 206, 213

Flexible — 75, 170, 177

Flexions — 98

Focus — 38, 72, 73, 80, 88, 90, 96, 136, 197, 199, 200, 202, 204, 206, 207, 213

G
Gladysz, Jerry — 20

Grounding — 87, 94, 98, 127

I
Impatience — 38

Intensity — 64, 70, 74, 75, 77, 84, 96, 207

In-line skating — 155, 157, 159, 161

J
Jump turn — 130, 131

K
Kick turn — 71, 138

L
Late Bloomers — 169, 178

M
Martini Tree — 60

Mayer, Jean — 8, 10, 13, 33, 39, 44, 52, 54, 83, 90, 98, 99, 116, 165, 180

Moguls — 59, 71, 80, 105-107, 113, 115

Motor skill development — 156

Mugleston, Jeff — 8, 16, 180

Muscle involvement — 87, 97

N
Natural Athletes — 157

Natural stance — 113, 114, 132

O
Ostrich stop — 129

P
Peak performance — 73, 74, 198, 214

Performance zone — 73

Plan — 200, 201, 203, 204, 213

Pole plant — 109, 110

Porpoise turn — 130

Position — 25, 48, 54, 72, 87, 92, 97, 99, 155, 205, 207, 211

Powder — 28, 59, 71, 75, 89, 96, 123, 124, 126, 128-131, 133, 140-143, 148, 156

S
Self-preservation — 172

Separation anxiety— 147, 153

Simultaneity of foot action — 141

Skate boarding — 157

Social interaction — 156, 162

Soul skier — 31, 32, 35, 37, 39

Soul-skier effect — 73

Stagg, Chris — 29

T
The Art Of Skiing — 10, 36, 37, 38, 49, 215

The Taos experience — 50, 88

Timing — 99, 133, 134, 140, 163, 190

Traverse — 71, 115, 123, 139

Trees — 39, 59, 60, 70, 71, 80, 83, 84, 96, 99, 107, 109, 124, 136, 137

Turning — 60, 87, 89, 90, 95, 96, 130, 133, 186

V
Veth, Alain — 8, 15

Versatile — 72, 138, 155

Visual Imagery — 198-200, 202

W
Weight distribution — 99

Weighting — 98, 113

Z
Z-shaped turn — 140